NORWAY

POCKET GUIDE

Charcoal Broiled STEAKS ♀100 m

ER POT

DIAMANT Restaurant

BROOKLANN

JOE'S BURGERS Restaurant

WATE

NE

ARTS & CULTURE

MON 28
Space disco
featuring
Music

88 A TO Z INFO

⌐

SHOPPIN

Shopping
around
be f

⌐ ♀ MAP

ATE BRIDGE ♀100 m ⬏ SHARE

LIKE

Sailing under the Golden Gate Bridge today, it is interesting to consider that engineers once thought it impossible to span the Golden Gate Strait at this point, because of the depth of the water (318ft/ 97 meters, at its deepest point) and the powerful tidal rush.

The city authorized studies for a bridge in 1917, but it was 1933 before the first shovel turned under the gaze of master engineer Joseph B. Strauss (no relation to the famous waltz composer). Four years later the bridge opened at a cost of $35 million and the lives of 11 construction workers. Today the bridge

Q

INSIGHT ⊙ GUIDES

SPAIN

≡ 🖹 INTRODUCTION

88 EXPLORE F

EX

🗺 EXP

♀ 58.00

RIDA

This new edition of Insight Guide Florida is a comprehensive, full-colour travel guide packed with inspiration and information. It includes everything from colonial Fort West and

♀ 58.00

FRANCE

This brand new edition Insight Guide to France features outstanding full-colour photography and hundred new photographs. Insight Guide illuminating explorations of all the places to go

♀ 138.00

LUCIA Pocket Guide

one of the most luscious Caribbean is lushly forested, easy to hunt by Pocket Guide...

♀ 58.00

Walking Eye
mobile app

Discover the world's best destinations with the Insight Guides Walking Eye app, available to download for free in the App Store and Google Play.

The container app provides easy access to fantastic free content on events and activities taking place in your current location or chosen destination, with the possibility of booking, as well as the regularly-updated Insight Guides travel blog: Inspire Me. In addition, you can purchase curated, premium destination guides through the app, which feature local highlights, hotel, bar, restaurant and shopping listings, an A to Z of practical information and more. Or purchase and download Insight Guides eBooks straight to your device.

TOP 10 ATTRACTIONS

HEDDAL STAVE CHURCH
One of the finest of Norway's 29 stave churches. See page 34.

THE FJORDS
See the spectacular Hardanger, Sogne and Geiranger fjords on a boat trip. See pages 49, 56 and 58.

PULPIT ROCK
Climb to the top for stunning views over the Lysefjord. See page 40.

SVALBARD
Colourful cabins in this remote Arctic archipelago, the most northerly part of Norway. See page 77.

NORTH CAPE
This dramatic cliff is the northernmost point in mainland Europe. See page 73.

HARDANGERVIDDA
The mountain plateau is now a national park. See page 54.

JOTUNHEIMEN NATIONAL PARK
Perfect for summer hiking and winter skiing. See page 57.

OSLO
Norway's capital offers great shopping, fine dining and a wealth of art and culture. See page 25.

LOFOTEN ISLANDS
Stay in a cabin on these islands in Norway's far north. See page 67.

NORTHERN LIGHTS
The natural phenomenon of the *aurora borealis* is not to be missed. See page 86.

A PERFECT TOUR

Bergen

Fly into Bergen and explore the historic Hanseatic Quarter, Bryggen, then take the Fløibanen funicular railway to Mount Fløyen for gorgeous views. In the evening, sail out of Bergen on the Hurtigruten Coastal Voyage for its northbound journey.

Day 3

Trondheim

Arrive in the medieval city of Trondheim and pay a visit to the Nidaros Cathedral, Scandinavia's largest, where Norway's patron saint St Olaf the Holy is buried. For an altogether more worldly pursuit, Trondheim also has excellent shopping.

Day 4

Arctic Circle

Cross the Arctic Circle by ship and arrive at Bodø, surrounded by beautiful mountain scenery. Take a tour to Saltstraumen, the world's strongest maelstrom, before continuing on to the Lofoten Islands in the evening, disembarking at Stamsund for a night in a *rorbu* (fisherman's cabin).

Day 2

Geiranger and Ålesund

Spend the day on board ship admiring the spectacular landscape, including the Geirangerfjord. In the afternoon make a stop and stroll around the Art Deco town of Ålesund, repeatedly voted Norway's prettiest.

IN **NORWAY**

Day 6

Troll Fjord
Continue by bus to Svolvær, the hub of Lofoten, and take a boat trip to the magical Troll Fjord, surrounded by sheer cliffs with magnificent waterfalls. In the evening rejoin the Hurtigruten Coastal Voyage, sailing towards Tromsø.

Days 8–9

North Cape
Passing Hammerfest, the northernmost town in the world, stop at Honningsvåg for a few hours' excursion to otherworldly North Cape, a steep cliff rising 307 metres (1,007ft) from the ocean. Fly back from Kirkenes, the final stop on the Hurtigruten voyage, the following day.

Day 5

Scenic Å
Take a bus to the tiny community of Å in the very south of the islands, which is worth a visit for its scenic location and its two interesting museums depicting life on the Lofoten Islands in times gone by.

Day 7

Tromsø
Visit Tromsø, the capital of the Arctic, home to the Arctic Cathedral, the Polar Museum and the Polaria Centre, before sailing on to the far north of Norway.

CONTENTS

INTRODUCTION

The most accurate observation made about Norway is that it is a land of contrasts: majestic mountains tower above mysterious fjords; harsh winters are relieved by often glorious summers; and long polar nights give way to the radiant midnight sun. Norway offers the visitor a beguiling mix of tradition and modern convenience, spectacular nature and city delights.

LAND AND PEOPLE

Situated in the northwest corner of Europe, on the Scandinavian peninsula, Norway is bordered by Sweden to the east, Skagerrak, the North Sea and the Atlantic Ocean to the south and west, the Arctic Ocean, Barents Sea, Finland and Russia to the north. Covering 385,252 sq km (148,747 sq miles) with a latitude ranging from 57° north to 72° north, from south to north, Norway is one of the largest countries in Europe, but has a population of only 5.2 million, or 16 people per sq km (41 per sq mile). The northernmost point of mainland Europe is situated in Norway and one-third of the country lies above the Arctic Circle, including the islands of Jan Mayen, Svalbard and Bear Island *(Bjørnøya)*.

Large parts of Norway are covered by mountain chains, or high plateaux such as Hardangervidda, the largest in Europe at 11,900 sq km (4,600 sq miles). The coastline mostly consists of fjords, islands, islets and skerries, while the east, bordering Sweden, has large forests and lakes. This leaves only three percent as arable land, and traditionally

Bear Island

Bear Island, discovered by Dutch explorers Willem Barents and Jacob van Heemskerk in 1596, is now a protected nature reserve.

many Norwegians had to combine farming with fishing to make ends meet and survive the harsh climate. The sea has shaped the land, not just physically, but in creating the nation of Norway, ancient and modern, from the seafaring Vikings, the long-standing trade in fish and fish products and the more recent discovery of oil in the North Sea at the end of the 1960s. Norway is still one of the world's greatest exporters of fish and seafood, as well as the third-largest supplier of oil.

Cross-country skiing is a favourite Norwegian pastime

Some 86 percent of the people living in Norway today are ethnic Norwegians, a North Germanic people. The Sami, one of the world's indigenous peoples, mostly hail from four counties, concentrated in the north, with Kautokeino and Karasjok as the two main centres, both in the northernmost county, Finnmark. In recent years, Norway has also seen an influx of immigrants and workers from a number of countries and over 13 percent of the population is either of foreign descent or foreign born.

NORWEGIAN LIFESTYLE

High taxes have meant excellent benefits provided by the state and a high standard of living. Although the cost of living is comparatively high in Norway, the quality of goods and services is usually first-rate. The majority of modern Norwegians live in or near one of the main cities – Oslo, Bergen, Stavanger/Sandnes or

Trondheim – but more often than not they will own or at least rent a *hytte* (cottage or cabin) out in the countryside to which they can escape for weekends and holidays.

The Northern Lights are a spectacular sight

You could almost imagine all that energy of the average *nordmenn*, or 'men of the North', to be caffeine-induced. Norway has the second-largest per capita consumption of coffee in the world, downing 160 litres (35 gallons) per person per year. Despite this, Norwegians tend to be health-conscious – research shows that more than 70 percent practise some form of sport or take regular exercise. In summer, nothing seems to give people more pleasure than to head out into the wilds for the day, hiking boots on, packed lunch made, and quite possibly the youngest family member bundled up on a parent's back – the taste for nature, fresh air and open spaces starts early. In winter the hiking boots are swapped for cross-country skis, and *långrænn* (cross-country skiing) beats downhill skiing in the popularity stakes here any day. Whether they are city-dwellers or country types, Norwegians take health and fitness seriously at any time of year, taking full advantage of the country's topography and size. There are 2,600km (1,600 miles) of coastline for canoeing, kayaking, sailing or fishing, high mountain peaks for rock-climbing and mountain biking in summer, or Alpine skiing in winter, and endlessly varied scenery of fjords, high plateaux and forests providing awe-inspiring hikes.

MIDNIGHT SUN AND NORTHERN LIGHTS

The scenery of Norway is one of its main draws for visitors. The stunning contrasts of lofty mountains and glaciers, snow-covered even in the height of summer, the deep gorges of the fjord land-scape with crystal-clear bright blue waters, cascading waterfalls and endless open vistas, are enough to take the breath away of even the most jaded of world-travellers. Views such as that from Pulpit Rock, *Preikestolen*, with a sheer drop of over 600 metres (1,970ft) down to the Lysefjord below, or the Lofoten Wall, as the dark, forbidding cliff wall of the Lofoten Islands is known, are sights that have converted many a visitor into a firm Norway enthusiast. The tiny hamlet of Geiranger, with only 300 inhabitants, receives around 700,000 visitors a year, who come to enjoy the magic and splendour of narrow Geirangerfjord, without the place seeming too crowded. There is always a sense of space and room to roam in Norway.

The climate may be harsh and unpredictable, but that is part of the charm. The weather tends to be best from May to August, the most popular time to visit, but the further north you go, the colder it gets. The summer season is short and intense, often with temperatures in the mid-20s°C (70s°F) in the south and up to around 20°C (68°F) in the far north. This is the time to enjoy the midnight sun, a phenomenon best seen north of the Arctic Circle. Depending on latitude the sun does not move below the horizon from May/June until late July/early August.

Norway, although still most popular during the summer months, is also becoming more of a year-round destination, not least thanks to another spectacular natural phenomenon, the Northern

Etiquette

Always take your shoes off when entering someone's home or you will be guilty of your first (and possibly worst) faux pas.

One of Thor Heyerdahl's vessels in Oslo's Kon-Tiki Museum

Lights, *aurora borealis*, best spotted in October, February and March. The latter are also great months for skiing and other winter sports.

CULTURE AND TRADITION

Despite centuries of Danish and Swedish rule and cultural influence, Norwegians forged a national identity of their own early on. Norway has had numerous cultural ambassadors, who have all helped to put it on the world map. Writers Henrik Ibsen and Bjørnstjerne Bjørnson, artist Edward Munch and composer Edward Grieg are the best known internationally; lovers of crime fiction might add the names of Scandinavian noir authors Jo Nesbø and Karin Fossum. During the era of exploratory expeditions Roald Amundsen and Fritjof Nansen further enhanced Norway's reputation, as did Thor Heyerdahl more recently – to which the Polar Museum in Tromsø and the Kon-Tiki Museum in Oslo are testament.

Although old traditions are still cherished, Norway is one of the most progressive countries in the world in terms of environmental issues, gender equality and laws allowing same-sex marriage. The country's first female prime minister, Gro Harlem Brundtland, first took office in 1981. Norway is also not afraid to go against the current, as has been the case with its whaling policy, which the country still allows on a quota basis; or when voting on two occasions against joining the European Union.

A BRIEF HISTORY

The Viking ancestors of the Norwegians, the Sami peoples, the Danes and the Swedes have all shaped the history of Norway, just as the last Ice Age shaped the landscape, making the country what it is today. For a nation that has spent such a large part of its history influenced by, and in union with, its two Scandinavian neighbours, Norway's identity and culture have nonetheless refused to become submerged, remaining strong until – and since – the country achieved independence in 1905.

EARLY HISTORY

Norway began to emerge from the ice cover of the last Ice Age around 14,000 years ago, and it is estimated that certain parts of the country have been inhabited for at least 11,000 years. The coastline was the first area from which the ice receded enough for human settlement to occur, and by 9300 BC people had settled even as far north as Magerøya, near the point of the North Cape, in Finnmark. The oldest Stone Age findings in Norway, from what is known as the Komsa culture, dating from 7000 BC, are found in the very north, in Troms and Finnmark, while in southern Norway the Nøstvet, and later the Fosna, cultures settled. These were early hunter-gatherers; agricultural settlements only began to occur around 4000 BC.

Viking finds

The Viking Ship Museum in Oslo houses some of the best Viking finds including the Oseberg ship, discovered in a burial mound at a farm called Oseberg, near Tønsberg, west of Oslo. The ship dates from around AD 800.

The Sami, one of northern Europe's indigenous peoples, settled in northern Norway some estimate as long as 4,000 years ago, migrating from the east to northern Russia, Finland, Sweden and Norway.

THE VIKING ERA

From the end of the 8th century until the middle of the 10th, Scandinavian people began to play a much greater role in Europe and even further afield – the Viking era had begun. While Swedish Vikings mostly headed east in their exploration and raids, Norwegian and Danish Vikings headed west, setting up trading posts and settlements along the way. Norwegian Vikings colonised the Shetland and Orkney Islands, large parts of Great Britain and Ireland, the Faroe Islands and Iceland. They even ventured as far as Greenland and modern-day Newfoundland in Canada. Although the Vikings

⊘ OLAF THE HOLY

Olaf Haraldsson (995–1030), the man who completed the unification of Norway, was a descendant of Harald Fairhair, who first began the unification process in the 9th century. Converting to Christianity while in England, Olaf's mission was not only to Christianise the country, but also to unify it. Long before this was accomplished he fell in battle at Stiklestad, but soon miracles were reported to occur near his tomb, today found beneath the Nidaros cathedral in Trondheim, and a cult surrounding him sprang up. Olaf went on to become the patron saint of Norway. The Pilgrim's Route to Trondheim across Norway reopened in 1997 and was declared a European Cultural Route in 2010.

initially simply carried out planned attacks on coastal or riverside communities, they soon began to spend winters at strategic points, thus making their settlements more permanent, and by the mid-9th century they were controlling large areas of northern Europe, with a centre at Jorvik, modern-day York in the United Kingdom. This was the beginning of the close ties Norway has kept with Britain over many centu-

Olaf the Holy

ries of seafaring and trade. When the Vikings first became a force to be reckoned with, Norway as we know it today was divided into many smaller fiefdoms, where chieftain was often pitted against chieftain and petty, warring factions fought it out among themselves for a power base. The first king tradition-ally credited with beginning the unification of Norway is Harald Fairhair, or Harald Hårfagre, who is believed to have ruled the coastal and southern areas of Norway from AD 872–930.

UNIFICATION OF NORWAY

The Vikings travelled to many parts of Europe, coming into contact with different peoples and cultures and also with Christianity. Up until the 10th century, Norway had been pagan; the Vikings worshipping the Norse pantheon of gods. This began to change after Harald Fairhair's son, Håkon, known as Håkon the Good, adopted the Christian faith in Britain.

Peter Nicolai Arbo's *Håkon the Good* (1860)

However, Håkon chose not to impose his beliefs on his subjects by force and it was left to one of his successors, Olaf Haraldsson, known as St Olaf the Holy, who became the country's patron saint, to convert the people of Norway, and he was not afraid to use force in the process. It wasn't religion so much as further unifying the nation that drove Olaf, and he is the first king to have ruled most of modern-day Norway, including the north and inland to the east. He died in battle at Stiklestad, near Trondheim, in 1030, and after his death became revered as a saint. By the end of the century the Christianisation of Norway was complete and no other religion was allowed in the country.

DANISH INFLUENCE

The 13th century has come to be viewed as a Golden Age. During the rule of Håkon VI, the kingdom was further consolidated and Christianised, with the cities of Oslo, Bergen and Trondheim beginning to flourish. The Orkneys, Shetlands, Faroe Islands, Hebrides and Isle of Man all belonged to Norway at this point in history and there also existed a union with Greenland and Iceland. This was the time when the great kings' sagas in Norway and Iceland were composed, but notwithstanding this, the Viking era of chieftains and fiefdoms was at an end and in the unified kingdom all the sons of a king, including the illegitimate ones, had the same right to inherit their father's throne. This led to a period of civil war in Norway, as well as allegiances and intermarriage to try to secure the throne. When King Håkon VI married Margrethe, the daughter of the Danish king, his son Olaf became king of Denmark in 1376 and upon his father's death also king of Norway, in 1380. This was the start of a long period of unions in Scandinavia. In particular, Norway's union with Denmark was to last almost entirely unbroken until 1814.

The Black Death is believed to have arrived in Norway in 1349 on board a ship from Britain, and its effects were devastating, rapidly killing off some two-thirds of the population between 1349 and 1351. Norway was left weakened and depopulated, and entered a long period of decline. The Queen Mother, Margrethe of Denmark, in 1397 succeeded in uniting

⊙ STAVE CHURCHES

After the Christianisation of Norway in the 11th century, the early missionaries busied themselves with the construction of a number of churches across the formerly heathen lands. These so-called stave churches are medieval wooden structures and the name stems from the building technique of using load-bearing posts in timber framing. In the past there may have been as many as 2,000 stave churches across northern Europe, but only a handful remain today, the majority of which are to be found in Norway. Twenty-nine of these churches are still standing, most dating from the 12th century. Urnes stave church in Sogn og Fjordane is a Unesco World Heritage Site.

Norway, Denmark and Sweden, in the so-called Kalmar Union, a union that lasted almost 140 years, until Sweden seceded in 1536. Norway, on the other hand, stayed in union with Denmark for almost another 300 years.

During this period Norwegian self-rule and decision-making were further weakened, while Danish influence was strengthened. The Danish crown was represented across Norway by governors appointed by the Danish king. The late 16th to early 18th centuries were dominated by wars and the Norway–Denmark union lost territory to Denmark's archenemy, Sweden.

As elsewhere, the French and American revolutions inspired hopes for stronger national identity and there was a greater desire for Norwegian independence, but the future had other things in store for Norway before these hopes could be realised.

UNION WITH SWEDEN 1814–1905

When the union of Denmark and Norway was defeated in the Napoleonic Wars in 1814, Denmark was forced to cede Norway to Sweden, a move that was not at all popular in Norway, where the desire for an independent nation had grown stronger over the preceding four decades. The Norwegians decided to declare independence at Eidsvoll, and adopted their own constitution on 17 May 1814, a date still celebrated as Norway's national, or constitution, day, a major public holiday. The Swedes retaliated and a brief war ensued, but Sweden agreed to accept the democratic Norwegian constitution and a loosely based union with the country, on the condition that the Danish prince Christian Frederik, who had backed the Norwegians, gave up his claim to the Norwegian throne. This achieved, the Norwegian Parliament, *Stortinget*, agreed to elect the Swedish king as ruler of Norway on 4 November of the same year.

INDEPENDENCE

The tide of independence, however, could not be stemmed. In 1905, more than 90 years after first entering into the union with Sweden, it was dissolved without bloodshed. This had been preceded by several years of political unrest between the two countries, and Sweden finally recognised Norway's independence after some 250,000 signatures were collected to support the move. Even before independence, Norwegian cultural and scientific achievements began to blossom as never before, with writers such as Bjørnstjerne Bjørnson and Henrik Ibsen (who died the year after independence was declared), composer Edward Grieg and explorer Fridtjof Nansen bringing the world's attention to Norway in an unprecedented way.

World War II memorial in Ålesund

FOUNDATIONS OF THE MODERN SOCIETY

Norway remained neutral during World War I and it was during the early years of independence that industry started taking off on a more major scale, laying the foundations for the welfare state and modern Norwegian society. The growth of industry and the economy continued during the interim years, but during World War II, Norway's neutral stance could not be maintained, with Germany invading and occupying the country from 1940–5. A Norwegian Nazi,

Vidkun Quisling, collaborated closely with the German invaders, so much so that the word 'quisling' has come to mean 'traitor' or 'someone collaborating with an occupying force'. Many parts of Norway were severely affected by the war, and the northern towns of Narvik and Bodø, in particular, were heavily bombed. World War II and its aftermath put a seemingly permanent stop to Norway's aspirations to neutrality, and when Nato was formed in 1949 Norway was one of the first nations to join. In 1959 it also joined EFTA, the European Free Trade Association. Norway's fortunes took another unexpected turn when oil was discovered in the North Sea in the late 1960s. With the oil find, the already high standard of living improved further, and in a referendum in 1972 a small majority voted against joining what is today the EU, a decision that would be repeated more than 20 years later in 1994, when yet again the Norwegians said no to joining.

The 20th century was initially characterised by nation-building, followed by overcoming the hardships of war and finally by taking an active role in European and world politics, on a peace-keeping level. Modern Norwegian politics have been dominated by a long-standing labour tradition, with a mixture of social democratic and liberal values. This has stimulated industry, while also encouraging state intervention and the welfare state, through high taxes. A fiercely independent nation, Norway has maintained its tough alcohol policies and its defiant stance on whaling, a tradition that goes back many centuries, particularly in the north of the country. Norway has one of the highest standards of living in the world, in terms of education, income and life expectancy, and also ranks second in terms of gender equality, according to the World Economic Forum.

HISTORICAL LANDMARKS

9000 BC Earliest signs of settlements recorded in Norway.

4000 BC Farming settlements begin to spring up in southern Norway.

872–930 King Harald Fairhair begins the unification of Norway.

961 Håkon the Good, Harald Fairhair's son and the first king of Norway to adopt Christianity, dies in battle.

1015–28 Olaf II further unifies and Christianises Norway.

1030 Olaf dies in battle at Stiklestad. He later becomes the patron saint of Norway, known as Olaf the Holy.

1070 Building of the Nidaros Cathedral in Trondheim begins.

1349–51 The Black Death kills two-thirds of Norway's population.

1397–1536 Norway becomes part of the Kalmar Union with Sweden and Denmark.

1536–1814 Norway remains in union with Denmark.

1814–1905 Norway is united with Sweden after Napoleonic Wars.

1901 Norwegian government awards first Nobel Peace Prize.

1905 Norway becomes fully independent from Sweden.

1914 The country remains neutral during World War I.

1918 Norwegian women gain the right to vote.

1940–5 Germany occupies Norway during World War II.

1949 Norway joins Nato.

1968–9 Discovery of oil in the North Sea. Production begins in 1971.

1972 Norway votes against joining the EU.

1981 Gro Harlem Brundtland becomes Norway's first female prime minister.

1994 Norway votes for the second time against joining the EU. Hosts the Winter Olympic Games in Lillehammer.

2011 Terrorist attacks perpetrated by Anders Behring Breivik in Oslo and on Utøya Island result in 77 deaths.

2013 Erna Solberg becomes Norway's second female Prime Minister.

2015 The Norwegian Lutheran Church allows gay couples to marry in church.

2018 In January, Erna Solberg forms a new coalition government of the Conservative Party, the Progress Party and the Liberal Party.

The historic wharves on the
River Nidelva, Trondheim

WHERE TO GO

From the understated charm of the white-painted villages of the southern coastline, to the stark, barren beauty of the Arctic north, Norway has a lot to offer intrepid travellers, particularly those with a penchant for the great outdoors. The cities of Oslo, Bergen, Stavanger and Trondheim are big enough to be interesting and varied, but small enough to get around and feel at home in, and even here nature is never far away. The landscape is ever-changing in a country that runs for 1,752km (1,089 miles) from north to south, encompassing mountains, forests, glaciers, lakes, tundra and, most famous of all, the Norwegian fjords.

OSLO

The Norwegian capital, founded in 1048, lies on the waters of the Oslo Fjord with a bustling harbour. Mountains serve as a backdrop and the Great Outdoors never seems far away even in the centre, with its leafy parks. The main artery, Karl Johans Gate, partly pedestrianised, runs through the centre, connecting many of the major sights.

CENTRAL OSLO

With 673,000 inhabitants, **Oslo ❶** is by far the most populous city in Norway, but the centre is compact and easy to get around. The best way to see it is on foot, and the **Central Station ❹** (Sentralstasjon) makes a good starting point since this is also where you find the main tourist office. Outside the station is the start of **Karl Johans Gate**, affectionately known just as 'Karl Johan', the 1km (0.6-mile) -long main street that runs through the centre up to the Royal Palace. The first half is a pedestrianised

The imposing Norwegian Parliament building

zone, running uphill to the **Cathedral**  (Domkirke; Stortorvet 1B; www.oslodomkirke.no; Sat–Thu 10am–4pm; Fri 4pm–6am; free) only two blocks from the station. The cathedral may appear unassuming from the outside, but it's worth a peek inside for the colourful ceiling and stained-glass windows, designed by Emmanuel Vigeland. Surrounding the cathedral is an old bazaar dating from the middle of the 19th century. Today it's full of quirky shops, selling trendy clothes and jewellery, and there are cafés and restaurants with outdoor seating in summer. The pedestrianised part of Karl Johan is lined with shops ranging from the tackiest of souvenir stands to designer labels.

Starting at the **Norwegian Parliament** (Stortinget; www.stortinget.no; guided tours in English mid-Jan–mid-June and Sept–Nov Sat 10am, 11.30am; mid-June–mid-Aug Mon–Fri 10am, 1pm; free), Karl Johan becomes a wide boulevard. The parliament building has been the seat of the National Assembly since 1866, when Norway was still in union with Sweden, and it is partly open to the public. Eidsvolls Plass, parallel to Karl Johan, has lovely fountains playing in summer and an ice rink in winter. It leads down to the **National Theatre** (Nationaltheatret), with **Oslo University** (Universitet) opposite. Straight ahead at the end of Karl Johan, facing the parliament, lies the serene **Royal Palace** ❶ (Kongelige Slottet; www.royalcourt.no; guided tours mid-June–mid-Aug, in English daily at noon, 2pm, 2.20pm and 4pm; tickets sold online at www.ticketmaster.no or tel: 81-53 31 33; some last-minute tickets available at entrance), a large building in muted yellows with clean Nordic lines, surrounded by the abundant parklands of the Slottsparken.

Across Slottsparken, another of Oslo's main thoroughfares, Henrik Ibsens Gate, leads to **Munkedamsveien**, a street with stroller-friendly pavements, nice shops, cafés and bars, running down to **Filipstad Brygge** and **Tjuvholmen**, both part of an ambitious waterfront development project. Next door is **Aker Brygge** ❷, a former shipyard that has been completely regenerated, turning into one of Oslo's best places to shop, eat and drink. It houses more than 70 shops and 40 eateries from fast food to fine dining and, situated right on the harbour, is positively buzzing on summer nights. A walk along the harbour promenade offers good views over the harbour and fjord where you can pick up sightseeing boats and cruises. Not far away, on Rådhusplassen, lies the **Nobel Peace Center** ❸ (Nobels Fredssenter; www.nobelpeacecenter.org; 10am–6pm May–Aug daily, Sept–Apr Tue–Sun), telling

Christmas market

In the weeks leading up to Christmas, Rådhusplassen, in front of the City Hall and the Nobel Peace Center, plays host to a large Christmas market, selling handicrafts from all over Norway.

the history of the prize and offering exhibits on war, peace and conflict resolution. Close by is the **City Hall** (Rådhuset). A short walk east is **Akershus Fortress and Castle G** (Slott og Festning; fortress area daily 6am–9pm; free; the castle was closed for restoration at the time of writing; changing of the guards 1.30pm), a 13th-century fortress built to protect Oslo from attack. On the other, Western side of the Pipervika bay, the **Fearnley Museum of Modern Art** (Astrup Fearnley Museet; www.afmuseet.no; Tue–Wed and Fri noon–5pm, Thu noon–7pm, Sat–Sun 11am–5pm), located in a modern waterside building designed by Renzo Piano, presents works by such artists as Olafur Eliasson, Damien Hirst, Jeff Koons, Charles Ray and Andy Warhol.

To the east lies another magnificent modern structure overlooking the bay the **Opera House H**, which offers a varied programme of classic and contemporary opera and ballet. Continuing northwest, **Christiania Square**, one of the oldest squares in Oslo, is surrounded by quaint buildings, some dating from the 17th century. Akersgata leads back to Karl Johans Gate, north of which, on Universitetsgaten, is the **National Gallery I** (Nasjonalgalleriet; www.nasjonalmuseet.no; Tue–Wed and Fri 10am–6pm, Thu until 7pm, Sat–Sun 11am–5pm), with a great collection of works by Norwegian artists. As of 2020, the collections of the National Gallery and several other museums will be housed in the new National Museum for Art, Architecture and Design which is being constructed at the site of the former Vestbanen train station.

EAST AND SOUTH OSLO

Former working-class and immigrant areas in east Oslo, such as Rodeløkka, Grünerløkka and Grønland, have become hip and happening. The most interesting is Grünerløkka, easily reached from the National Theatre by tram (trikken) No. 13, which runs right through the district. This is a place to amble, soak up the atmosphere and check out the quirky boutiques, international grocery stores, organic food shops, unusual eateries and quiet residential areas. Thorvald Meyers Gate is the main street and Birkelunden park with the Paulus Church is pleasant.

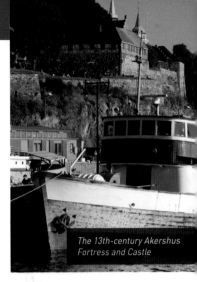

The 13th-century Akershus Fortress and Castle

Southeast of Grünerløkka, through Sofienberg Park, past the Sofienberg Church, lies the area of **Tøyen**, home to some excellent museums, clustered together and surrounded by the lush **Tøyenhagen Botanical Gardens**. The Palaeontological, Zoological, Geological and Natural History Museums can all be found here (times vary). The gardens themselves are worth a visit, especially for the aromatic herb garden. Opposite the garden entrance lies another of the city's best museums, the **Munch Museum** (Munchmuseet; www.munchmuseet.no; mid-May–early Sept daily 10am–5pm, early Sept–mid-May until 4pm, Thu until 9pm), housing over 28,000 works by the artist Edvard Munch. There are plans to relocate the museum to brand new premises with more exhibition space. The new venue, which will house the collections of the Munch Museum and the former Stenersen Museum (Stenersenmuseet), is scheduled to open at Bjørvika, next to the Opera House, in 2020.

Continuing south (tram No. 18 or 19) will bring you to **Ekebergparken** (www.ekebergparken.com; daily 24 hours; free), a city park which is home to a fascinating array of sculptures,

One of 200 statues in Vigeland Sculpture Park

including works by Salvador Dalí and Auguste Rodin, as well as numerous contemporary installations.

WEST AND NORTH OF THE CITY

The Majorstua area (tram No. 19 from the National Theatre) also has interesting shops and cafés. From the Majorstua tram and underground station it's a short walk to the **Vigeland Sculpture Park** (Vigelandsparken; www. vigeland.museum.no; daily 24 hours; free), with more than 200 statues made by Gustav Vigeland. His former studio is now the Vigeland Museum (Tue–Sun noon–4pm; free). The City Museum and a museum dedicated to ice-skating are here, too. A 30-minute stroll down Frognerveien, with grand old houses, cafés and restaurants, takes you back to the centre of town.

Oslo's other museum area is the **Bygdøy Peninsula**, which can be reached by boat (No. 91; services Apr–Oct) from the City Hall pier. Bygdøy is home to the **Norwegian Folk Museum** (Norsk Folkemuseum; www.norskfolkemuseum.no), an indoor/outdoor venue devoted largely to rural culture; the **Fram Museum** (Frammuseet; www.frammuseum.no) housing Fridtjof Nansen's polar sailing ship Fram; and the **Kon-Tiki Museum** (Kon-Tiki Museet; www.kon-tiki.no), opposite which is the **Maritime Museum** (Norsk Maritimt Museum; www.mar museum.no; all museum times vary).

To the north, **Holmenkollen** (www.holmenkollen.com), with the ski jump, arena and world's oldest ski museum, is one of Oslo best-loved attractions, and nearby **Frognerseteren** has some of the best views of Oslo and the bay.

THE SOUTH AND SOUTHEASTERN BORDERLANDS

Southern Norway is characterised by a rocky coastline teeming with islands, islets and skerries, many of which are popular summer holiday spots for Norwegians. The coast is dotted with pretty towns and villages with white-painted houses. Further inland lie some of Norway's richest farmlands, while to the east forests spread across the border with Sweden.

SOUTHERN COAST

Travelling out of Oslo, along the Oslo fjord, is **Tønsberg ②**, some 100km (62 miles) south. On the surface Tønsberg does not appear to have much of interest, but this town, the oldest in Norway, has a rich history going back over 1,100 years and is worth a stop for its 13th-century castle ruins and Viking-era grave mounds. It is also famed as the home of *Jarlsberg* cheese. **Oslo Torp** airport is nearby and there are direct connections by ferry from Sandefjord to Strömstad in Sweden.

Passing Sandefjord and Larvik on the E18, the main Oslo–Stavanger highway, **Kragerø** is the first picturesque white-washed village of note, followed by **Risør**, known as the 'White town on the Skagerrak'. The former was the favourite haunt of artists such as Edvard Munch, while the latter has beautifully preserved 17th-century houses. Both have a variety of accommodation and restaurants.

Heddal Stave Church

Continuing south, **Arendal** is one of the larger towns along the coast, worth a visit for its old district, **Tyholmen**.

Grimstad, another white-painted coastal town further south, is said to have the most hours of sunshine in Norway. In the 19th century, Grimstad was one of the greatest shipbuilding centres in the world, and the Maritime Museum (May–Sept Mon–Sat 11am–5pm, Sun 1–5pm) provides fascinating insights into this aspect of the town. West of Kristiansand lies Norway's southernmost town **Mandal**, followed by the country's southernmost point, **Lindesnes**, with a lighthouse and museum (www.lindesnesfyr.no; mid-Apr–mid-Sept daily, Mar–mid-Apr and mid-Sept–mid-Oct Wed–Sun, mid-Oct–Feb Sat–Sun, times vary).

KRISTIANSAND

Kristiansand ❸ is the largest city in southern Norway and the fifth largest in the country. Situated at the southern end of

Norway, 330km (205 miles) from Oslo, it is the hub of the south with ferry connections to Denmark. The town centre is known as **Kvadraturen** and encompasses most of the sights of note, including the **Fish Market** (Fiskebrygga; daily) near the small harbour along the quayside. The market is a good place to soak up the atmosphere and grab a nice, fishy lunch at one of the eateries.

One of the most prominent features of Kristiansand is the **Christiansholm Fortress**, an imposing structure from 1672, set right on the seafront promenade, amid extensive lawns, attracting sun worshippers in summer. Heading east from the fortress, the city has its own beach, **Bystrand**, also popular when the weather allows. Away from the seafront, five blocks along Kirkegata, lies the city's **Cathedral**, the third largest in Norway, with capacity for 1,800 people. A short walk northeast is the old part of town, **Posebyen**, with buildings dating from the 17th–19th centuries. The 14 blocks of low-rise wooden houses are perfect for a quiet stroll.

One of the main attractions of the region lies 9km (5.5 miles) east of the centre. **Kristiansand Zoo and Amusement Park** (see page 94) is a major draw for the whole family.

EXPLORING INLAND

Inland from the coast, 80km (50 miles) west of Oslo, **Kongsberg**, founded in 1624, is known for its old silver mine. The last mine was closed in 1957, but there is plenty of silver history to experience and explore here. At Hyttegata 3, the fascinating **Mining Museum** (Norsk Bergverksmuseum; www. norsk-bergverksmuseum.no; mid-May–late Aug daily 10am– 5pm, late Aug–mid-May Tue–Sun noon–4pm) has a wealth of information on the era, and it is also possible to visit the **Royal Silver Mines** on guided tours, about which the museum has more information.

Continuing west along the E134 you will reach the largest preserved stave church in Norway, **Heddal Stave Church** (www.heddalstavkirke.no; May–late Sept daily 10am–5pm). There is a café and an outdoor museum.

To the south, in Telemark, the **Telemark Canal**, a 105km (65-mile) stretch of lakes and a man-made canal, connecting Skien and Dalen through 18 locks, is a picturesque boat journey, taking a leisurely 11 hours (www.visittelemark.com).

North of Dalen, along highway 37, **Rjukan**, in the shadow of Telemark's highest peak, Gausta, has become something of an outdoor activities and adventure sports centre. This is the place to try Alpine and cross-country skiing, ice climbing and ski-sailing in winter, bungee-jumping, rock climbing, archery and horse riding in summer, among many other things (www.visitrjukan.com).

A cable car at Rjukan, beneath Gausta Toppen, Telemark's highest peak

SOUTHEASTERN BORDERLANDS

The region of Østfold, between the Oslo fjord and the Swedish border, is an area steeped in history, as evidenced by its strong fortifications, hailing from a time when relations between Norway, Sweden and Denmark were less neighbourly and far more belligerent.

Fredrikstad, 90km (56 miles) southeast of Oslo, on the Oslo fjord and River Glomma, is perhaps the best preserved fortress town in Scandinavia. The **Kongsten Fortress** dates back to 1685, when Norway was in union with Denmark, whose arch-enemy Sweden was only a stone's throw away. **Gamlebyen** is the name of the old town, also dating from the 17th century, with a number of historic buildings, a drawbridge, moat and fortifications. Nearby **Halden**, almost waving distance from Sweden, less than 10km (6 miles) away, is another town with a formidable fort. **Fredriksten Fortress** (www.fredrikstenfestning.com; museum late-May–Aug 11am–5pm, grounds 24 hours year-round; guided tours available) sits on a hilltop overlooking Halden itself. Built in 1661, in its heyday it withstood six Swedish sieges without ever being captured. At the southeasternmost point of Norway lies the **Ytre Hvaler** national marine park.

STAVANGER AND AROUND

Stavanger ❹, in the county of Rogaland, is Norway's third-largest city, including nearby Sandnes and the metropolitan area. It was near here that the unification of Norway began with Harald Fairhair, and in more modern times Stavanger was often the last that the 900,000-odd Norwegians who emigrated to North America saw of their nation. The sea has played a prominent part in Stavanger's history – there are strong links with Britain across the North Sea and the city is also the headquarters of the

Norwegian oil industry. The fjord scenery in the surroundings is some of the country's most spectacular, and Pulpit Rock on the Lysefjord is something that every visitor must see.

CENTRAL STAVANGER

Most of the sights in Stavanger are concentrated within easy walking distance of each other. In the very centre of town, near the railway station, lies **Breiavatnet**, a lovely lake with fountains, surrounded by pleasant buildings, some of which serve coffee and cakes. Just to the north of Breiavatnet is the city park and **Stavanger Cathedral** (Domkirken; June–Aug daily 11am–7pm, Sept–May Tue–Thu and Sat 11am–4pm; free), built in 1125 in Anglo-Norman style. The tourist information office

⊙ GOING WEST

Organised emigration from Norway to North America began in 1825, when the ship *Restauration* set off from Stavanger for New York City. Upon arrival it was impounded for exceeding the declared passenger limit – one passenger had given birth during the 98-day voyage – and the captain had to spend two weeks in jail for the offence. Between 1825 and 1925 well over 800,000 Norwegians, roughly one-third of the population, left for North America, and today there are some 5 million Norwegian-Americans, ie more than there are Norwegians in Norway itself. The majority settled in the Midwest, with Minnesota, Wisconsin and the Dakotas having the highest percentage of Norwegian descendants. In North Dakota, for example, more than 30 percent of the population have Norwegian roots. Some 40,000 people still speak Norwegian in the home across North America, and Norwegian culinary traditions and cultural expressions live on, on the other side of the Atlantic.

Detail of Stavanger Cathedral

can be found just behind the cathedral (Domkirkeplassen 3; tel: 51-85 92 00). From here, a short walk leads down to the harbour on the inlet of **Vågen**. Stavanger's waterfront is a bustling place, lined with restaurants, bars and cafés, as well as the boats moored in the guest harbour. It is a nice place to eat alfresco in summer, and also the site of Stavanger's annual summer food festival, *Gladmat*. Northeast, behind the harbour, lies an area of cobbled streets, unusual shops and boutiques, with an ever-so-slightly bohemian feel to it.

This area is also home to **Valbergtårnet** (mid-June–mid-Aug Mon–Wed and Fri 10am–4pm, Thu until 6pm, Sat until 2pm), a mid-19th-century watchtower built to protect Stavanger from fires. Sadly the original watchtower, which was made of wood, burnt to the ground and was replaced by the current one, built of stone. A few blocks east of Valberget, the quayside is home to the **Petroleum Museum** (Norsk Oljemuseum; www.

A colourful street in Stavanger

norskolje.museum.no; June–Aug daily 10am–7pm, Sept–May Mon–Sat 10am–4pm, Sun 10am–6pm), dedicated to all things oily. You can even experience life on an oil rig here and find out about Norway's recent history as an oil producing nation. Geoparken, next to the museum, has everything for the modern child, from skateboarding facilities to sand volleyball.

OLD STAVANGER

On the western side of the Vågen inlet lies what remains of the **Old Town**, 173 well-preserved wooden buildings mostly from the turn of the 18th century. Where the old town begins, along the quayside lies the **Maritime Museum** (Sjøfartsmuseet; www.museumstavanger.no; Tue–Fri 11am–3pm, Sat–Sun 11am–4pm), and further along the same quay, the **Norwegian Emigration Centre** (Det Norske Utvandrersenteret; www. emigrationcenter.com; temporarily closed to visitors but the genealogy service is still operating online), charting the history of Norwegian emigration.

Another unusual museum in the old town is the one dedicated to the canning industry. The **Canning Museum** (Norsk Hermetikkmuseum; Øvre Strandgt. 88 and 90; www.museum stavanger.no; Tue–Fri 11am–3pm, Sat–Sun 11am–4pm) is located in an old canning factory and there are former workers' cottages also open to the public in summer. In its heyday in 1925, Stavanger had 58 such factories, the majority of them canning sardines. The old town in general is lovely for a stroll around the pretty wooden houses with their well-tended gardens. Bear in mind, though, that this is not a living museum: many houses are inhabited by Stavanger citizens, who don't always appreciate visitors peeking too closely through their windows.

⊙ BLACK GOLD

Norwegian oil exploration began in 1968, but it wasn't until the summer of 1969 that one company, on the verge of giving up, discovered a huge oil field upon completing its last wellbore. Production commenced at the *Ekofisk* field on 15 June 1971 and it's still believed to have the largest reserve of oil almost 40 years later, despite Norway having opened up 51 active oil and gas fields across the Norwegian continental shelf of the North Sea since then. In 2001 the field was given the status of cultural heritage monument. Oil and gas comprise 47 percent of Norway's exports, making it by far their largest export commodity. The industry employs some 80,000 people in total and Norway is now the world's tenth-largest oil exporter. Stavanger, with its good harbour, airport and close proximity to the oil fields, has been Norway's oil capital since the early days of exploration.

ART AND CULTURE

In many parts of Stavanger a number of seemingly random cast-iron figures can be spotted. The **Broken Column** by English artist Antony Gormley is a huge project consisting of 23 cast-iron sculpted figures, all 1.95 metres (6ft 4in) tall and cast, like all his figures, from his own body. The first one is at Rogaland Art Museum, 41 metres (135ft) above sea level, the final one stands on rocks *below* sea level. They can be found in the cathedral churchyard, in a swimming pool, a car park, a school yard, and there is even one in a private home.

Another cultural project, which has been running since 2008 when Stavanger was designated European Capital of Culture, is **Norwegian Wood**, focusing on Stavanger as Europe's largest timbered city – it has more than 8,000 wooden houses. It includes 15 building projects, designed with an environmentally friendly ethos.

AROUND STAVANGER

The town of **Sandnes**, 12km (7.5 miles) to the south, is considered part of the Stavanger/Sandnes metropolitan area. From here it is a short drive to one of Norway's most spectacular fjords and perhaps the bestknown view in the country – the **Lysefjord** seen from **Pulpit Rock** ❺ (Preikestolen). The Lysefjord and Pulpit Rock mountain lodge, which opened in 2008, can both be reached by car or boat from Sandnes, or by ferry and bus or car from Stavanger via Tau, from May to September. From base

Summer festivals

Summer is festival time in Stavanger with more than 100 events, including full-moon concerts, an international tattoo convention, shooting championships, and much more (www.regionstavanger-ryfylke.com).

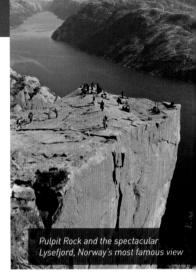

camp at the mountain lodge a marked trail leads up to the rock itself, a two- to three-hour climb that can be very steep in places and should only be attempted if you are reasonably fit and wearing strong shoes. Those who do make the hike are rewarded by stunning panoramic views, but the 604-metre (1,982ft) -high cliff is not for the faint-hearted. Lying face-down at the edge of the cliff, spotting the sightseeing boats far

Pulpit Rock and the spectacular Lysefjord, Norway's most famous view

below, is very popular if slightly vertigo-inducing. Those of a less adventurous or energetic bent can choose to view the rock and the fjord from a fjord cruise, which can be taken year-round, whereas the hiking trail is only safe for five months of the year (Rødne Fjord Cruise does three-hour cruises on the Lysefjord; www.rodne.no).

Another, more strenuous, hike is that to **Kjerag mountain**, famed for its 5-sq-metre (54-sq-ft) boulder, plugged between two rocks. This requires a three-hour hike each way, from the visitor centre at Øygardstølen.

The area north of Stavanger has numerous fjords, both large and small, plus islands and skerries, perfect for exploring by boat; there are many ferry services available (www.kolumbus. no). Another option is to explore by bike. The **EuroVelo** runs through 15 coastal municipalities in the county of Rogaland and carries on all the way to Bergen (www.eurovelo.com). **Karmøy**, one of the largest islands, is a summer paradise with quaint timber houses, beautiful beaches and Viking-era grave mounds. Harald Fairhair, who began the unification of Norway, lived on the island, and there is a medieval church in Avaldsnes dedicated to St Olaf. North of Karmøy lies **Haugesund**, a North Sea port with a number of interesting historical buildings.

BERGEN AND AROUND

Bergen ➏, capital of the county of Hordaland, is Norway's second-largest city and has a long history. From the end of the 13th century it was an important Hanseatic trading port with strong links to Germany. Situated on the North Sea, surrounded by peaks, it's known as 'the city of seven mountains', although in reality there are more than seven summits surrounding the city. Bergen has also become the gateway to many of Norway's most spectacular fjords, such as Hardangerfjord to the south and Sognefjord to the north.

A pretty street in Bergen

THE SIGHTS OF CENTRAL BERGEN

Like many of Norway's main cities, Bergen is situated on the seafront and the centre is concentrated around the harbour, known as the Vågen inlet. **Strandkajen** runs along the southern side of the harbour and it's from here that many sightseeing boats set off. From Strandkajen there are also great views of Bryggen, on the opposite side of the quay. Following Strandkajen you reach **Torget** Ⓐ and the **Fish Market** (hours vary), one of the liveliest fish markets in Europe, selling fruit, vegetables and souvenirs as well as a vast variety of fish and seafood. It's perfect for picking up a quick bite at lunchtime, and many of the stalls provide rustic wooden benches for customers' use. There is also a small pier with restaurants and bars, jutting out into Vågen. Opposite the Fish Market is the tourist information centre and the starting point for most of the sightseeing bus tours.

> ### Bergen Theatre
>
> Henrik Ibsen and Bjørnstjerne Bjørnson were both directors at the renowned Bergen Theatre, Norway's oldest. The theatre season runs September–May (tel: 55-54 97 00; www.dns.no).

North of the Vågen inlet lies **Bryggen** Ⓑ, an area of medieval merchants' houses from Bergen's Hanseatic period that has been a UNESCO World Heritage Site since 1979. As quite a few of the buildings have been turned into shops selling all things Norwegian from knitwear to elk souvenirs, you can see what they are like inside. The **Hanseatic Museum** (Hanseatiske Museum; www.museumvest.no; daily May and Sept 9am–5pm, June–Aug 9am–6pm, Jan–Apr 11am–3pm) in one of the best preserved buildings in Bryggen, furnished in the style of the times, gives a fascinating glimpse into Hansa life. Nearby, the **Schøtstuene** was the merchants' assembly hall and a school for their apprentices.

Continuing along the quayside, past Bryggen, in the Bergenshus area, you find **Håkon's Hall** (Håkonshallen; www.bymuseet.no; daily mid-May–mid-Sept 10am–4pm, mid-Sept–mid-May noon–3pm), a 13th-century royal residence, the largest secular medieval building in Norway, although much reconstructed after World War II damage. Beside it is the **Rosenkrantz Tower** (Rosenkrantztårnet; www.bymuseet.no; Jan–mid-May Sun noon–3pm, mid-May–mid-Sept daily 9am–4pm, mid-Sept–late Dec Tue–Sun 11am–3pm), added to Håkon's Hall in the 1560s, which has permanent and special exhibitions.

There are a number of old buildings along Sjøgaten, the road north along Skuteviken Bay, such as the Sandviksboder warehouses for drying and storing fish, which is worth a peek. The **Sandviken** area nearby is another interesting part of old Bergen, and Sandviksveien road leads up to **St Mary's Church** (Mariakirken), the oldest medieval church still in use (its splendid pulpit is a Baroque addition). Services here were still held in German until the late 19th century.

From St Mary's Church, Øvregaten runs along the back of the Bryggen merchants' houses to the nearby **Fløibanen Funicular**

⊙ THE HANSEATIC LEAGUE

The Hanseatic League was the major trading force in the North and Baltic seas from the mid-14th to the 16th century. It began in northern Germany, and was an alliance of merchant traders who operated much like guilds, looking after each other's interests, arming their own ships and gaining favourable concessions from governments. Hanse merchants flourished around the coasts, and where they were strong, in such cities as Lübeck in Germany, they also established political autonomy. At their height, there were trading posts in some 170 towns and cities from London to Moscow. Their influence was seen in the architecture, which can be seen from King's Lynn in the UK to Bergen, and also in Scandinavian languages, which borrowed from the North German merchants.

Medieval Bryggen is a World Heritage Site

Railway that goes up to Mount Fløyen for gorgeous views across Bergen (www.floibanen.no; Mon–Fri 7.30am–11pm, Sat–Sun 8am–11pm). The journey to the top takes only 5–7 minutes, and there is a café open daily in summer, at weekends during the rest of the year. Fløibanen is best enjoyed in good weather, and since Bergen's climate is extremely unpredictable, if the sun's out, it's best to take advantage.

CENTRAL BERGEN AND NORDNES PENINSULA

Between the Fish Market and the Fløibanen Funicular lies the **Church of the Holy Cross** (Korskirken), originally medieval but now largely Renaissance; and a short walk east, the **Cathedral** (Domkirke), which, despite its medieval origins, has been rebuilt five times because of fires. In the same street, Kong Oscars gate, lies the unusual Leprosy Museum (Lepramuseet). Bergen once had a huge concentration of

The Fløibanen Funicular Railway on its way up to Fløyen

leprosy patients, and the bacillus was discovered here in 1873 by Armauer Hansen. Running parallel is Kaigaten, bordered by Lille Lungegårdsvann, the attractive city park, with a small lake and a pavilion. The grand **Grieghallen** concert hall lies on the other side of the park. Externally, it resembles a grand piano; internally, the acoustics are marvellous.

Southwest of Lille Lungegårdsvann, in the university district, are a number of interesting museums: the Natural History Museum (Naturhistorisk) set in a botanic garden; the Cultural History Museum (Kulturhistorisk) with information on stave churches; and the Maritime Museum (Sjøfartsmuseet). Heading northwest, onto **Nordnes Peninsula**, along Strandgaten, is New Church (Nykirken), the first church in Bergen to be built as Lutheran, rather than converted from Catholicism. At the tip of the peninsula lies the **Aquarium** (Akvariet; www.akvariet. no; May–Aug daily 9am–6pm, Sept–Apr Mon–Wed 10am–4pm, Thu and Sat–Sun until 6pm), with a tunnel where you can get extra close to the sharks.

AROUND BERGEN

Troldhaugen (http://griegmuseum.no; daily May–Sept 9am–6pm, Oct–Apr 10am–4pm; guided tours available) was the home of composer Edward Grieg and his wife Nina. It is situated a

20-minute bus ride south of Bergen, on a peninsula overlooking Nordsåsvatnet inlet. The house is just as he left it, with his piano in working order. There is also a small museum and a concert hall that can be visited; during summer there are concerts and recitals (summer daily, winter selected Sun). The grave of Edward and Nina Grieg is embedded in the rock face near the house. On a clear day the views from Troldhaugen are lovely.

The Grieg Museum is one of several museums that form part of the **KODE Art Museums and Composer Homes** complex (tel: 53-00 97 04; http://kodebergen.no/en; May–Sept daily 11am–5pm except KODE 3 until 6pm, Sept–May Tues–Fri 11am–4pm, Sat–Sun 11am–5pm, closed 1 and 17 May),

⊙ EDVARD GRIEG

Norway's most famous composer, Edvard Grieg (1843–1907), was partly of Scottish descent. His father's grandfather hailed from Aberdeenshire in Scotland in the 18th century and four generations of Griegs (then spelled 'Greig'), including Edvard's father, held the post of British consul in Bergen. Edvard, on the other hand, decided on a different career path. Growing up in a musical home, he enrolled at the conservatory in Leipzig, Germany, where he finished his studies in 1862. He is perhaps best known for having composed the music for his friend Henrik Ibsen's play *Peer Gynt* in 1874–6. Among his other illustrious friends were Franz Liszt and Pyotr Tchaikovsky. Grieg set to music the lyrics of several poems by Goethe, Ibsen, Kipling and others, and wrote a number of songs. He married his first cousin Nina in 1867 and their home, Troldhaugen outside Bergen, is now open to the public. He died aged 64 after a long period of illness.

which opened in 2013 and is one of the largest art and design museums in Scandinavia. As well as the homes of composers Edward Grieg, Ole Bull and Harald Sæverud around Bergen, there are four buildings in the centre of town – imaginatively named KODE 1, KODE 2, KODE 3 and KODE 4 – which showcase art from the Renaissance to the contemporary, as well as musical instruments and fine crafts.

Several of the mountains surrounding Bergen can be reached by funicular or cable car. The summit of the 643-metre (2,109ft) Ulriken mountain can be reached by a cable-car trip, the **Ulriken643 Panorama Tour** (Easter–mid-Oct daily 9am–9pm, mid-Oct–Easter Tue–Sun 10am–5pm). Buses take visitors from the Fish Market to the cable car for stunning views across the city, islands and fjordlands beyond. There are 15 different hiking trails and circular routes when you get to the top, and other activities to choose from include climbing, abseiling and paragliding, as well as winter sports; and there is also a good restaurant.

Fantoft Stave Church (Fantoftveien, Paradis, 6km/4 miles south of the city centre; bus stop and car park at Birkelundsbakken; mid-May–mid-Sept daily 10.30am–6pm) is one of the few stave churches to be found within the limits of a large city. The original was constructed in the village of Fortun in Sogn county in 1150 and moved to its current location in 1883. It was burnt down in 1992 in an arson attack, but has been beautifully rebuilt as it was before the fire.

HARDANGERFJORD AND VOSS

The **Hardangerfjord**, the third-longest fjord in Norway, lies 75km (47 miles) southeast of Bergen. Boat trips can be arranged from Bergen harbour for the length or part of the fjord, or as part of one of the popular Nutshell Tours, which do a **Hardanger in a Nutshell** (www.norwaynutshell.com), taking in the fjord and surrounding areas. There are a number of sights, natural and man-made, alongside or near the fjord and along the smaller fjords connected to it. In the south, **Folgefonn Glacier**, Norway's third-largest ice field and a national park, offers summer skiing, snowboarding and sledding. Nearby, the picturesque town of **Rosendal** has Norway's only baronial mansion, dating from 1665. On the opposite side of the Handangerfjord, heading north, lies **Norheimsund**, worth a visit for its grand old hotel, as well as its scenic location. Hotel Sandven (see page 137) is more than 150 years old and has been beautifully restored over 15 years by Tron Bach, who spent a small fortune returning it to its former glory. The hotel is packed with antique furniture and had splendid views over the fjord and town – the latter seems to have sprung up almost entirely around the hotel, which was built with royal consent. The café and bar are open to non-guests. The hotel is surrounded by

Voss is the place to come for adventure sports

historic buildings and even has a mini-museum of old carriages in what used to be the court house.

The area between Nor-heimsund and Bergen, following highway No. 7, **Tveitakvitingen**, is well known for cross-country skiing in winter, and many chalets dot the landscape.

Further inland along the fjord, in the village of Utne, the **Hardanger Folk Museum** (www.hardanger ogvossmuseum.no; May–Aug daily 10am–5pm, Sept–Apr Mon–Fri 9am–3pm) features a medieval log house and general store among other things, and there are traditional Hardanger boats in the boathouse. On the Sørfjorden arm of the main fjord, **Kinsarvik** has one of Norway's first stone churches, dating from around 1250 and nearby **Lofthus** is home to Grieg's hut, which the composer used as a retreat. These days it's part of the garden of Hotel Ullsvang. All three villages can be reached by the regular ferry service plying the Hardangerfjord.

Crossing the fjord and travelling north on Highway 13, you reach the town of **Voss**. It has successfully marketed itself as Norway's adventure sports capital and lives up to the name. Voss has a history dating back to medieval times, with an ancient stone church and a folk museum, but these days the enthusiasts who flock to the town are mostly looking for chills and thrills of the extreme kind. Voss organises an annual extreme sports festival for a week every June (www.visitvoss. no), attracting large numbers of adrenalin junkies. If you're feeling adventurous this is the place to try paragliding, para-sailing and bungee-jumping, whitewater rafting, horse riding and a number of winter sports.

CENTRAL NORWAY AND THE WESTERN FJORDS

The central part of Norway has some of the country's most understated, as well as its most spectacular, landscapes. By the Swedish border to the east lie quiet forests and sedate farmlands. Moving west the landscape gradually changes into one of glaciers, high plateaux and lofty mountains, including the country's highest peaks. Finally in the far west the dra-matic peaks meet the sea, in what has become Norway's most famous natural scenery, the fjords.

THE CENTRAL EAST

The landscape of southeastern Norway is characterised by lakes and forests, reminiscent of the Swedish countryside. The area is rich in history with many fortresses and fortifications going back to the time when Sweden and Norway had less than neighbourly relations. **Kongsvinger**, 110km (68 miles) northeast of Oslo, is dominated by an imposing fortress on a hill overlooking the town, and the so-called Vinger Royal Road running through town was the main route in the early Middle Ages for pilgrims from Sweden on their way to St Olaf the Holy's tomb at Trondheim. **Eidsvoll**, some 70km (43 miles) north of Oslo and west of Kongsvinger, made its name in history when the Norwegians declared inde-pendence here in 1814. **Eidsvollbygningen**, the house where it all happened, is now a museum (www.eidsvoll1814.no; May–Aug daily 10am–5pm, Sept–Apr Tue–Fri 10am–3pm, Sat–Sun

11am–4pm). Following the E6 highway north of Eidsvoll, the next town of interest is **Hamar**, 66km (41 miles) away. Hamar lies on the shores of Norway's largest lake, **Lake Mjøsa**, and there is a sandy beach right in the town itself. Also on the lake is the world's oldest operating paddle steamer, *Skibladner*, which still runs each summer season. The ruins of Hamar's medieval cathedral, now with a glass cathedral built over the original ruins, are worth a visit. Nearby **Lillehammer** is known for hosting the 1994 Winter Olympics. You can visit the Norwegian Olympic Museum, and take a chairlift to the top of the Ski Jumping Arena. If you are not feeling sporty, there is the Maihaugen Open-air Museum of rural life and a good art gallery. Continuing north from Lillehammer along Highway E6 it is some 170km (106 miles) to Norway's oldest national park, **Rondane**, founded in 1962, home to wild reindeer,

⊙ THE OSLO TO BERGEN RAILWAY

The Bergen Line, the highest mainline railway line in northern Europe, runs for 496km (308 miles), between Norway's two main cities. It crosses the Hardangervidda plateau at 1,237 metres (4,058ft), and the highest station is Fisne at 1,222 metres (4,008ft). It was originally opened from Bergen to Voss in 1883 and then from Voss to Myrdal in 1907. The line passes some of the most scenic areas in Norway – the Hallingdal valley, the ski resort of Geilo and the Hallingskarvet plateau. The journey takes seven hours in total and the train makes a special stop at the highest station in case anyone should wish to nip out for a photo or some fresh, but nippy, air. The station of Myrdal, about halfway through the journey, is where another famous railway begins – Flåmbanen, which runs from Myrdal at 881 metres (2,890ft) down to Flåm at sea level.

and encompassing the cross-country skiing Troll Trail. The road passes through the beautiful **Gudbrandsdalen valley** with quaint farmhouses, steeped in history. There is also the chance to try out whitewater rafting on the Sjoa River.

THE MOUNTAINOUS CENTRE

The rail journey from Oslo to Bergen passes some of central Norway's most varied scenery on its way across the country. The valley of **Hallingdal**, around 100km (62 miles) north of Oslo, is well known for its traditional culture and folk music. At the northern end of the valley, **Gol** has one of Norway's best preserved stave churches, dating from 1216. Fifty km (31 miles) southwest, **Geilo**, between Hemsedalsfjella mountain and the Hallingskarvet plateau, is one of Norway's best downhill ski resorts. For less wintry exercise, the **Navvies' Road** (Rallarvegen), a former works access road during the construction of the Oslo–Bergen railway line, is now one of Norway's most popular cycling routes, starting at **Haugastøl** on scenic Ustevatn, 22km (14 miles) southwest of Geilo. The main stretch runs for 92km (57 miles) from Haugastøl to Flåm.

Another way to reach Flåm is via the Flåmbanen railway (www.visitflam.com) from Myrdal – one of the most attractive rail journeys in the world. The 20km (12.5-mile), hour-long train ride takes in majestic mountains, spectacular waterfalls and deep ravines, before emerging at Flåm on the Aurlandsfjord. Work began on the line in 1923 and took almost 20 years to complete. Today it is mostly a tourist route, with guiding in several languages and occasional photo stops.

On Highway No. 7, designated as a National Tourist Route, travelling southwest from Haugastøl, you reach **Hardangervidda National Park** (Nasjonalpark), Norway's largest, covering 3,422 sq km (1,321 sq miles). The vast area is popular for hiking and fishing in summer or cross-country skiing in winter, and there are numerous overnight shelters within the park. Hardangervidda has some of the world's largest wild reindeer herds roaming free, and there is plenty of other wildlife and birdlife to enjoy. The **Hardanger Nature Centre** (http://hardangerviddanatursenter.no; daily Apr–mid-June and late

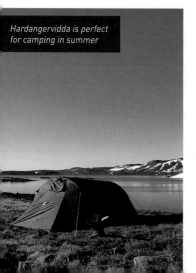

Hardangervidda is perfect for camping in summer

Aug–Oct 10am–6pm, mid-June–late Aug 9am–7pm) off route 7 near Eidfjord, has lots of information about the park, a good restaurant and can organise tours.

Also near Eidfjord, **Vøringsfossen Waterfall** is one of the most splendid waterfalls in Norway, dropping 182 metres (597ft), of which 145 metres (476ft) is a sheer drop straight down into Måbødalen valley below. The

Scenic routes

The Norwegian tourist board has designated six different routes as national tourist routes – roads that pass through some of the best scenery in Norway. These include: Lofoten, Helgeland, Rondane, Old Strynefjell, Sognefjell and Hardanger tourist routes (www.visitnorway.com).

hotel near the fall does great hot chocolate and cakes. **Eidfjord** itself, at the end of the fjord of the same name, an arm of the great Hardangerfjord, has become a popular centre for different outdoor activities including adventure sports and ice climbing in winter (www.hardangerfjord.com). The Eidfjord branches out into another arm, home to the small community of **Ulvik**, perched on the waterfront. It's worth having a look at the old church with original rose paintings from the area, as well as a 12th-century oil painting. The fabulous **Brakanes Hotel** on the waterfront (see page 137) is good for an evening drink on the terrace and there is plenty to see and do in the area (www.visitulvik.com).

For those really wanting to go back to nature, the **Hardanger Basecamp** (www.hardangerbasecamp.com) at Osa, a 15-minute drive from Ulvik, does Stone Age living and survival courses, and serves great waffles in the café. The Hardanger area is famous for apples, which have been grown there for centuries, and four apple-growing farms have banded together to create the **Hardanger Saft- og Siderfabrikk** (www.hardangersider.no)

producing juice, cider and apple brandy. There are pre-booked guided tours with tastings and information about the production process, and there is a restaurant with lovely views.

THE WESTERN FJORDS

Travelling north from Ulvik, the **Sognefjord** is the largest fjord in Norway and the second longest in the world, branching out into a number of arms, such as **Aurlandsfjord**, with the little community of **Aurlandsvangen**. The scenery here on a sunny summer day goes beyond the breathtaking. None of the scenic fjord communities has more than 300–400 permanent inhabitants, but in summer they swell enormously with visitors coming to enjoy the landscape. For the best views, drive to the **Stegastein lookout**, above Aurlandsvangen, a wood and glass structure with a sheer drop and a vertigo-inducing view. Norway's 2005 addition to the UNESCO list, the **Nærøyfjord**, the country's narrowest, can also be visited on a tour boat or regular ferry to Gudvangen. Undredal, en route to Gudvangen, has an excellent stave church. The main road from Aurlandsvangen to Lærdal passes through the Lærdal tunnel, the longest road tunnel in the world at 24.5km (15 miles), another tremendous feat of Norwegian engineering. Just after the tunnel, route 37 leads off to **Borgund**, which has a famous stave church (see page 19). Continuing across another arm of the Sognefjord, the **Årdalsfjord**, you come to **Sogndal**, the main hub of the Sognefjord.

Sogndal is a good base for exploring the area and planning excursions and activities. Just north of Sogndal, along yet another fjord arm, the **Lustrafjord**, another of Norway's medieval stave churches can be visited at **Urnes**. This is the oldest in the country (built in 1150) and the only one on the UNESCO World Heritage list. The fjord communities around Lustrafjord are worth a stop: **Gaupne** for its medieval church, **Marifjøra**

for a pleasant fjord beach and **Solvorn** for the oldest family-run hotel in Norway, Walaker Hotel, which has been in the capable hands of the Nitter family for more than 300 years.

Another national tourist route, Highway 55, runs along the Lustrafjord and up to **Jotunheimen National Park**, which covers some 3,500 sq km (1,350 sq miles) and is home to Norway's two highest mountains, **Galdhøpiggen** at 2,469 metres (8,100ft) and **Glittertinden** at 2,452 metres (8,087ft). This is prime hiking country, and also popular for skiing, glacier walking, rafting and riding as well as spotting elk, pine martens, lynx and golden eagles. The name means 'Home of the Giants' and stories of trolls and giants abound.

On the other side of Highway 55, to the west, lie two other national parks of note, **Jostedalsbreen** and **Breheimen**, which has well-marked hiking trails and protects a number of endangered animal and plant species. The former is home to the largest glacier in Europe, Jostedalsbreen Glacier. One of the highlights of the park is to take a (pre-booked) guided walk on **Nigardsbreen Glacier**, an arm of Jostedalsbreen. This involves harnesses, crampons and warm gloves even in summer. You need a certain level of fitness to undertake the hike, and a good head for heights, but the rewards are stunning views over pristine scenery, and the guides are very experienced. In summer

Ålesund is Norway's largest fishing town

the Glacier Bus runs from Sogndal to the visitors' centre, **Breheimsenteret** (tel: 57-68 32 50; www.jostedal.com), which has information on both parks.

Further north along the fjord landscape and coastline lies the beautiful city of **Ålesund ❼**, set on a peninsula surrounded by fjords on three sides. After a devastating fire destroyed the majority of the buildings in 1904, it was reconstructed in Art Nouveau style. The **Art Nouveau Centre** (Jugendstilsenteret; www.jugendstilsenteret.no; May–Sept Tue–Wed and Fri–Sun 10am–5pm, Thu until 8pm, Oct–Apr Tue–Wed and Fri–Sun 11am–4pm, Thu free until 8pm) is well worth a visit for information on the city's reconstruction, as well as for the centre itself, housed in a beautifully preserved pharmacy building at Apotekergata 16. The **Aalesunds Museum** (www.sunnmoremuseum.no; hours vary) is also interesting, with displays on shipping, fishing and sealing.

The town is also the gateway to one of Norway's most famous fjords, the UNESCO-listed **Geirangerfjord**. The Hurtigruten boats do a detour Ålesund–Geiranger–Ålesund on a day trip, taking some eight hours, and there are many other sightseeing boats that visit this 15km (9-mile) narrow strip of water, an arm of the Storfjord. The majestic scenery is further enhanced by waterfalls such as the Bridal Veil and the Seven Sisters. As you travel along you will see isolated farmsteads, some long abandoned, clinging to the sheer cliff walls, until you reach the tiny community of Geiranger itself, home to 300 souls, but swelled in summer by 700,000 annual visitors. Many choose to get off the boat at Geiranger and continue by road to another of Norway's most popular attractions, **Trollstigen**, the mountain road between Valldal and Åndalsnes with its many narrow hairpin bends and stunning scenery. **Molde** further north has one of northern Europe's best jazz festivals and many good jazz clubs, and is famous for its rose gardens.

TRØNDELAG AND NORDLAND

The region of Trøndelag begins where Norway starts to narrow and become the long, thin strip of land between the Swedish

⊘ NORWEGIAN TROLLS

Stories of the fearsome troll stem from Norse mythology and have developed over the centuries into sagas, legends and myths. Trolls were rumoured to have supernatural powers, to only come out at night, to live in the darkest of mountains or the deepest of forests. They were even said to have the ability to turn themselves into beautiful young maidens to lure away unsuspecting men; to live to be hundreds of years old or to melt in sunlight. Trolls have played a significant role in Norwegian and European culture – John Bauer painted them, Edvard Grieg named his home *Troldhaugen* after them, and Henrik Ibsen's *Peer Gynt* has a fair sprinkling of them. Looking at the imposing landscape of Norway, even today it is not hard to imagine trolls being alive and well here, feeling very much at home among the high peaks and frosty forests.

border and the sea. Further north, the region of Nordland narrows further, making it the longest region in Norway. Some 920km (572 miles) separate the city of Trondheim in the south to Narvik in the north. Trondheim is Norway's fourth-largest city, and, as the site of St Olaf the Holy's tomb, it is a long-standing spiritual, as well as commercial, centre. Further north, the cities of Bodø and Narvik are known for their fascinating wartime history, while the Lofoten Islands are the place to experience authentic Norwegian fishing culture.

CENTRAL TRONDHEIM

The centre of **Trondheim** ❽, known as **Midtbyen**, is almost entirely surrounded by water. River Nidelva encircles all but a small strip of land and Trondheimsfjord lies to the east of the centre, giving the city its lovely location. Trondheim was founded by a Viking king, Olav Tryggvason, as early as 997. Back then it was known as Kaupangen and later this was changed to Nidaros, a name that lives on in the city's famous cathedral. Trondheim has a great mixture of old and new buildings as many successive fires have ravished the city, the one in 1651 destroying 90 percent of the buildings.

The centre of Trondheim is best explored on foot. The main square, **Torget**, is a good place from which to set off, as it is also where you find the tourist information office (www.trondheim.no; tel: 73-80 76 60). Also in the main square is Trondheim Torg, a shopping complex with 75 shops. It is worth a visit not just for the retail opportunities, but for the unusual architecture, as some of the old wooden buildings have been incorporated into the mall.

A five-minute walk takes you up to Trondheim's main sight, the **Nidaros Cathedral** (Nidarosdomen; www.nidarosdomen. no; times vary), at Bispegata 5, the northernmost cathedral in the world and the largest in Scandinavia. The cathedral dates back to 1070, when it was built on the site of St Olaf the Holy's tomb, but has been much rebuilt over the centuries. The stunning stained glass is mostly from the early 20th century. During the Middle Ages the cathedral was part of the main European pilgrims' route, with many flocking to the site of St Olaf's tomb. In recent years the old pilgrims' route has been revived and in 2010 St Olaf's Way was declared a European Cultural Route by the Council of Europe. The Nidaros Pilgrim Centre behind the cathedral can supply information (www.pilegrimsgarden.no; tel: 73-52 50 00). Next to the cathedral are two of the city's best museums, the **Archbishop's Palace** (Erkebisgarden) and the **Army Museum** (Rustkammeret; www.forsvaretsmuseer.no/Rustkammeret; May–Sept Mon–Sat 10am–4pm, Sun noon–4pm; free), both housed in the oldest secular building in Scandinavia. The former displays crowns and sceptres and other regal items; the latter concentrates on World War II and the Resistance.

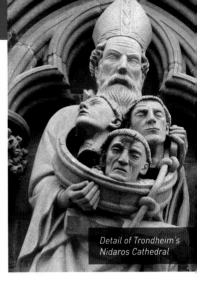

Detail of Trondheim's Nidaros Cathedral

The area around the cathedral is jokingly known as the Hallelujah Quarter, since it also contains an Evangelical church, a Catholic church and a Jewish synagogue, all in close proximity. Walking through the park behind the cathedral and following the river past the Pilgrims' Centre, you reach the **Old**

Town Bridge (Gamle Bybro) and the old town gates. There has been a bridge to the east river bank since 1681, but the current one dates from 1861. The east side of the Nidelva River is known as **Bakklandet**, where former workers' dwellings and old wharves have been turned into quirky shops and eateries. The views over the river and the colourful buildings are particularly good from the bridge at sunset.

Crossing back to Midtbyen you come to the **Church of Our Lady** (Vår Frues Kirke; daily 24 hours), Trondheim's second medieval church. Turning back towards the main square, at Munkegata 19, lies **Stiftsgarden**, the royal residence, where the royal family stays when in the area (https://nkim.no; June–late Aug guided tours only, Mon–Sat 10am, 11am, noon, 1pm, 2pm, 3pm, Sun noon, 1pm, 2pm, 3pm; closed during royal visits).

BEYOND MIDTBYEN

There are a number of interesting sights outside Midtbyen itself, not least several fortresses, built at a time when fortifications were necessary to protect it from its belligerent neighbour Sweden. **Munkholmen** is a small island in the Trondheimsfjord, where Benedictine monks built a monastery in the 11th century. By the mid-17th century the monks were gone and it had been turned into a prison and fortress. These days it's a popular recreational area and ferries run from Ravnkloa in Midtbyen from mid-May to mid-Sept.

Another fortress, **Kristiansten Fort** (Kristiansten Festning; museum mid-May–Sept Mon–Sat 10am–4pm, Sun noon–4pm, tel: 47-60 19 86 for guided tours; grounds daily Apr–May 8am–midnight, Sept–Mar 9am–midnight), built in 1681 on a hill to the east overlooking Trondheim, has great views across town and the surrounding fjord landscape. The road here runs past the University of Science and Technology, opened in 1910.

The former monastery on the islet Munkholmen

Solsiden, a shopping area with plenty of restaurants and nightlife to choose from, lies on the east side of Nidelva. The harbour area is being opened up and developed and is also home to **Rockheim** (Brattørkaia 14; www.rockheim.no; Tue–Wed and Fri 10am–4pm, Thu until 8pm, Sat–Sun until 5pm), a museum housed in an eye-catching modern building just north of Trondheim's central train station and dedicated to pop and rock music.

Take the Stavset bus No. 8 from Trondheim city centre to visit **Sverresborg Trøndelag Folk Museum** (Sverresborg Allé 13; www.sverresborg.no; June–Aug daily 10am–5pm, Sept–May Tue–Fri 10am–3pm, Sat–Sun noon–4pm), one of Norway's largest open-air museums, set around the ruins of a medieval castle. More than 60 buildings include one of the oldest stave churches in the country, dating from 1170, along with Sami huts and 18th-century town houses.

The Rockheim museum is dedicated to popular music

OTHER TRØNDELAG ATTRACTIONS

Don't be taken aback if the tourist board in Trondheim asks you if you would like to go to Hell. **Hell** is only half an hour's drive from central Trondheim and it's become a bit of a tourist attraction because of its name. If having your photo taken in front of the railway station of Hell is your cup of tea, this is the place for you. Somewhere of more interest and historical significance is **Stiklestad** some 90km (56 miles) northeast, where Olaf the Holy fell in battle in 1030. It has 30 historic buildings dating back to the 17th century, a medieval farm and holds an annual St Olaf festival in July (www.stiklestad.no).

Further to the south of Trondheim, the UNESCO World Heritage town of **Røros** should not be missed. An old mining town near the Swedish border, it was founded more than 300 years ago and it has an unusually large collection of 100 perfectly preserved wooden houses from the 18th century. A walking tour of

Røros will take in the majority of the sights and it is also possible to visit the Olavsgruva Mine with three centuries of mining history (www.roros.no). The very southernmost part of Trøndelag is home to **Dovrefjell-Sunndalsfjella National Park**, the only place in Norway where you can see the impressive musk ox.

The coastal landscape of Trøndelag is dotted with islands and skerries, somewhat understated and flatter than the fjords further south. Here tiny, quaint cottages and isolated settlements hug the seashore, some only reached by boat. This is an area perfect for cycling, fishing or island hopping (www.trondelag.com has more information).

⊙ UNESCO WORLD HERITAGE SITES

Since 1979 eight different parts of Norway's natural and cultural heritage have made it onto the UNESCO list of World Heritage Sites. Some, such as the Geirangerfjord and the old quarter of Bergen, are well known, whereas others have not yet become so renowned. The first two to be added were Bryggen, the medieval Hanseatic area of central Bergen, and Urnes stave church, in 1979. This was followed by the mining town of Røros near the Swedish border in south Trøndelag in 1980 and the rock paintings at Alta in Finnmark in 1985. Almost 20 years went by before UNESCO turned its attention towards Norway again when in 2004 the Vegaøyan Archipelago was listed, as well as the Struve Geodetic Arc in 2005. The latter is shared with a number of other countries. That same year the western fjords were also recognised, and the Geiranger and Nærøyfjord now also have UNESCO status. More recently, in 2015 the Rjukan-Notodden Industrial Heritage Site in Telemark county was added to the list.

Svartisen is Norway's second-largest glacier

NORDLAND

Travelling north from Trondheim into the next county, Nordland, you will reach the town of **Mo i Rana**, known for its ironworks, near which lies the **Svartisen-Saltfjellet National Park**. The second-largest glacier in Norway, Svartisen is popular for glacier walks in summer. Continuing north you will come to **Saltstraumen** ❾, 33km (20 miles) south of Bodø, where you can experience the strongest maelstrom, or whirlpool current, in the world. The speed of the water rushing through the narrow inlet between the Saltfjord and the Skjerstadfjord has been recorded at over 20 knots. Between June and August there are daily boat trips to get you closer to the tidal currents and to the birdlife – the rare sea eagle can be spotted here.

Bodø ❿, the administrative centre of Nordland, has fewer than 50,000 inhabitants. It's very manageable in size, and with

Norway's northernmost railway linking it to the rest of the country it's become a gateway to the region and the nearby Lofoten Islands. On the surface, the centre of Bodø may not have that much to offer, although it is beautifully situated between two fjords, the Saltfjord and the Landegodefjord. The city was heavily bombed during World War II and few buildings survived the onslaught, but the area around the harbour is picturesque and nice for a stroll. One of Bodø's main sights is the **Norwegian Aviation Museum** (Norsk Luftfartsmuseum; http://luftfartsmuseum.no; Mon–Fri 10am–4pm, Sat–Sun 11am–5pm), in a building shaped like a giant propeller, close to Bodø airport. It includes civil and military aviation history sections. Nearby Bodøsjøen, on the Saltfjord, has an open-air museum and a beach for the hardy outdoor enthusiast – temperatures rarely rise above 14°C (57°F).

Half an hour north of Bodø by car and ferry lies the scenic old trading post of **Kjerringøy**, and the whole area is good for hiking. Most of Nordland lies above the Arctic Circle, making this a good area to see the midnight sun in summer and northern lights in autumn and winter.

LOFOTEN ISLANDS AND NARVIK

From Bodø it's a four-hour boat journey to the port of **Stamsund**, on the remote and beautiful **Lofoten Islands** ⓫. The archipelago has six main islands and has been inhabited since Viking times. It has a 1,000-year history of cod fishing,

Private cell

An old shop in Å in Lofoten is one of the few places in Norway to have a private prison cell in the basement, hailing from a time when the lord of the manor had the powers to lock up the unruly who had been celebrating the end of the fishing season too hard.

and to this day Norway's most authentic fishing culture can be found here. Stamsund, on Vestvågøy in southern Lofoten, is a quiet old village where many of the old fishermen's cabins, *rorbuer*, have been converted into accommodation for visitors. These cabins date from the time when large numbers of fishermen would come across from the mainland for the annual cod fishing season. Stamsund is also renowned for its puppet theatre festival, and there are no less than three theatres in this village of only 1,100 people.

The road leading south from Stamsund and Leknes passes some of the islands' most stunning scenery – misty high peaks rising sharply from the water's edge, and the water itself, a dark turquoise with improbably white sandy beaches. Set amid this grandeur of nature is the **Lofotr Viking Museum** in Borg (www.lofotr.no; times vary), which also holds Viking feasts in summer. Continuing south, you reach the islands of Flakstadøya and Moskenesøya, the former with spectacular scenery and good accommodation possibilities in Flakstad and Ramberg. The latter is a haven for artists, particularly around **Reine**, which is also an arts and crafts centre. Reaching the southernmost tip of the island, make a stop at the oddly named little town of Å. This tiny community has two of the islands' best museums, offering better insights into island life and the history of Lofoten. The **Norwegian Fishing Village Museum** (Norsk Fiskevaermuseum; www.museumnord.no; mid-June–Aug daily 9am–7pm, Sept–mid-June Mon–Fri 10am–5pm), detailing life

Arctic Ski Pass

The Arctic Ski Pass is valid at four ski resorts in northern Sweden and Norway, including the ski slopes outside Narvik. See www.narvikfjellet.no for more information.

in the fishing community over the past 200 years; and the **Stockfish Museum** (Lofoten Tørrfiskmuseum; June–Aug daily), with displays and lively information on the processing and export of stockfish – a lot more interesting than it sounds. Å itself is appealing, with a quaint, old-world feel and a number of red-painted *rorbuer*.

A seaplane on the waterfront at Svolvær in the Lofoten Islands

Svolvær, on the island of Austvågøya, is the main town on the islands, with a pleasant harbour and a number of older buildings. From here there are popular tours of scenic **Trollfjorden**, a 40-minute boat trip away and surrounded by sheer cliffs with magnificent waterfalls. Nearby **Henningsvær** is a centre for rock climbing and unusual craft- and clothes shops (www.lofoten.info, tel: 76-06 98 00 for information about the islands).

When the LoFast Road opened in 2007, the Lofoten Islands were finally connected to the mainland, cutting journey times and making it a lot easier to get around.

Narvik ⑫, the last main town in Nordland before reaching Tromsø, is situated on the Ofotenfjord near the Swedish border. It is worth a visit mainly for its interesting World War II history. One of the fiercest battles in Norway between British and German armies was fought here in between April and June 1940, and a new modern **Narvik War Museum** (https://warmuseum. no; daily 10am–4pm) which opened in mid-2016 tells the story.

Next door to the museum is a small fish market with an accompanying restaurant. Narvik is also known for its railway, built at the turn of the 20th century to connect it with the mines in Swedish Lapland, since Narvik has an ice-free port year-round, thanks to the Gulf Stream.

THE FAR NORTH

Troms and Finnmark are the two northernmost counties of Norway, the latter reaching as far as the Russian border to the east. Both counties are situated above the Arctic Circle. Tromsø is the main city in Troms, whereas Alta has the highest population in Finnmark, although Vadsø is the capital. The far north is a sparsely populated area of outstanding natural beauty. It is also the traditional home of the Sami people, and Sami culture is particularly centred around the towns of Karasjok and Kautokeino.

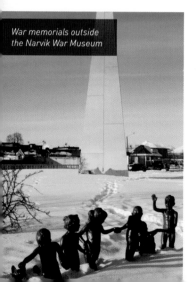

War memorials outside the Narvik War Museum

TROMSØ

The city centre of **Tromsø** ⑬ is situated on the island of Tromsøya. The main road from the south crosses the 1km (0.6-mile) Tromsø Bridge, an imposing structure that blends nicely with the landscape and links the island to the mainland. The Hurtigruten terminal, bus

station and tourist information office can all be found
in the same place, near the
quayside at Prostneset.
This is a good place to start
exploring the sights of the
city. Tromsø centre is nice
and easy to get around and
has a surprisingly large
number of old wooden
buildings that have survived
the ravages of World War II.

Bust of Roald Amundsen
at the Polar Museum

Following the quay-
side you get to the **Polar
Museum** (Polarmuseet;
https://en.uit.no; daily
mid-June–early Aug 9am–6pm, mid-Aug–mid-June 11am–
5pm) at Søndre Tollbodgate 11, which opened in 1978, 50 years
to the day after Roald Amundsen set off from the city on his
last expedition. Housed in an old customs house, the museum
depicts Amundsen's journeys, exhibits some of his paintings
and has a wealth of information on the history of Arctic trap-
pers and more. Be aware that the displays of seal clubbing are
graphic and may upset some people.

From the museum follow Bispegata to the start of Storgata,
one of the main streets and home to **Perspektivet Museum**
(www.perspektivet.no; Tue–Fri 10am–4pm, Sat–Sun 11am–5pm;
free), housed in a neoclassical manor house and focusing on
Tromsø's past and present. A few doors down, the Verdensteatret
theatre is one of the oldest in Norway and has the original decor
in the movie salon. The theatre organises a silent film festival
every September. Further along Storgata is the main square,

Stortorget, and a Catholic church. Further still is the Lutheran cathedral, and continuing right through the centre of Tromsø you reach the **Mack Ølhallen** (Mack Brewery; www.mack.no; brewpub Mon–Wed 11am–8.30pm, Thu until 00.30am, Fri until 1.30am, Sat 10am–1.30am; guided tours and beer tastings available), the northernmost brewery in the world ('Mack' is somewhat unfortunately pronounced 'muck'). There is also a beer hall, full of kitsch, including a life-size stuffed polar bear by the entrance.

Just past the Ølhallen lies the Tromsø Gallery of Contemporary Art, and then, down by the waterfront, at Hjalmar Johansensgaten 12, is **Polaria** (Polar Research Centre; tel: 77-75 01 00; www.polaria.no; daily mid-May–Aug 10am–7pm, Sept–mid-May 10am–6pm). Don't miss the feeding of the seals daily at 12.30pm in summer.

Across the bridge in Tromsdalen, the **Arctic Cathedral**, (Ishavskatedralen) built in 1965, is an unusual and daring structure in stark white, and in the shape of a massive triangle. It is open year-round, and in summer there are late-night concerts to coincide with the midnight sun.

TROMSØ TO THE NORTH CAPE

North of Tromsø, the **Lyngen Alps** (Lyngenalpene) mountain range, bordered by the Lyngen fjord on one side and the Ullsfjord on the other, is an area of high peaks, reminiscent of the Alps. The highest summit reaches 1,833 metres (6,014ft) and several glaciers can be found here. This remote region has a good mountain lodge open year-round, the Lyngen Lodge (www.lyngenlodge.com).

Crossing into **Finnmark**, Norway's northernmost county, **Alta**, with some 20,000 people, is the main population and administrative centre. Perhaps surprisingly for such a remote place, Alta is on the UNESCO list of World Heritage Sites (see

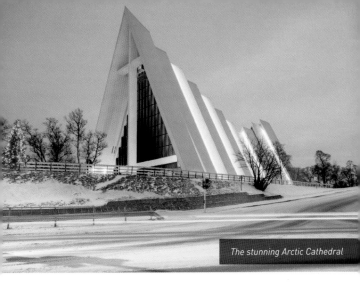

The stunning Arctic Cathedral

page 65). On the southern outskirts of Alta, at Hjemmeluft, as many as 5,000 rock carvings were discovered in 1972, dating back over 6,000 years. The carvings can be visited at the **World Heritage Centre for Rock Art – Alta Museum ⑭** (www. alta.museum.no; mid-May–early June and late Aug–mid-Sept daily 8am–5pm, early-June–mid-Aug daily 8am–8pm, mid-Sept–mid-May Mon–Fri 9am–3pm, Sat–Sun 11am–4pm).

Further north along the coast is **Hammerfest**, which prides itself on being the northernmost city in the world, although with only 9,000 inhabitants this might be stretching the definition of 'city'. However, by Norwegian law you only have to have more than 5,000 inhabitants to qualify. **Honningsvåg**, further north still, is in dispute with Hammerfest as to which is the northernmost city, but Honningsvåg has the advantage of attracting the tourists as a gateway to the **North Cape ⑮** (Nordkapp), on Magerøya island. Although not strictly speaking the very northernmost

Getting around by snowmobile in Varangerhalvøya

point of mainland Europe, since it's on an island, it is now renowned as such and pulls in the visitors accordingly. The journey across Magerøya to the North Cape takes under an hour and the landscape is starkly beautiful and barren. Honningsvåg is the main hub, but there are another four fishing hamlets on the island, three on the east coast and one on the west.

The North Cape itself, at latitude 71° north, has a large, modern visitors' centre, looking somewhat out of place in this landscape of natural beauty (www.nordkapp.no; May–Aug Mon–Fri 9am–8pm, Sat–Sun noon–7pm, Sept–Apr Mon–Fri 11am–3pm, to coincide with buses). The cliff plunges 307 metres (1,007ft) into the Barents Sea below, but it's not just the cape itself that is worth a visit. The scenery surrounding it is quite remarkable – barren at first glance, but home to some 205 different plant species.

In the Finnmark interior, **Karasjok** and **Kautokeino** are Norway's main centres for Sami culture, although all of Finnmark and several other counties have Sami communities. In Karasjok around 90 percent of the population speak Sami as a first language, and the area is home to more than 60,000 reindeer. Both towns are good places to find out more about Sami culture and traditions, and there are several cultural centres, including the **Sami Collections** (www.rdm.no; times vary) in Karasjok, an open-air museum. For more information about the Sami in the area, see www.visitsapmi.no. Be aware that here you are far from the sea, temperatures tend to be severe in winter and the average temperature in January in Karasjok is -17°C (1°F), although it can drop much lower.

In the far northeastern corner of Finnmark county, **Varangerhalvøya** is an area of outstanding natural beauty that is slowly opening up to tourism. The Hurtigruten boats make four stops along this peninsula, at Berlevåg, Båtsfjord, Vardø and Vadsø, on their way to their final stop at Kirkenes.

Between Berlevåg and Båtsfjord, the two small communities of **Kongsfjord** and **Veines** lie nestled on the Kongsøyfjord, an inlet from the Barents Sea. Like most places along this coastline, Kongsfjord is an old fishing village, where the

On safari at Kirkenes

Red king crab

fishery buildings have been recently restored. There is a quaint little shop, the Kongsfjord Landhandel og Café, mixing the kitsch and the quirky. Further out on a peninsula jutting into the fjord, Veines is a small collection of brightly painted houses, including a gallery displaying arts, jewellery and handicrafts, and the Kongsfjord Gjestehus (see page 140).

The landscape of the Varangerhalvøya itself is mesmerising, undisturbed and quiet even in the height of the Arctic summer, the roads empty with the exception of the odd roaming reindeer. You can hike and camp anywhere, but be sure to take a good map, a compass and provisions in this sparsely populated area.

South of Båtsfjord, on the **Syltefjord**, along a minor road, another cluster of former fishing houses lies amid stunning scenery. In summer the place comes alive, as some of the houses open up to visitors. One of the most unusual buildings is the **Stauran Art Café and Accommodation**, where they sell original Arctic stone art, hand-painted on pieces of rock, and offer accommodation in wooden cabins, individually designed in rustic style (see page 140). Syltefjord also has a small museum, and the Arctic Tourist tour company organises birdwatching and king crab safaris on the fjord and at sea (www.arctictourist.no). The birdwatching opportunities at nearby **Bird Mountain**, Fuglefjell, are seemingly endless, and you will be sure to spot puffins, cormorants and numerous other species.

The last main Norwegian town before the Russian border is **Kirkenes** (www.visitkirkenes.no). It is the end of the line for the Hurtigruten boats and the municipality borders both Russia and Finland. From here it is possible to make excursions to both, or for a taste of Russia in Norway, Kirkenes has a monthly Russian market, usually on the last Thursday of the month. Several museums depict Kirkenes' past as a frontier town. Nearby **Øvre Pasvik** national park has Norway's largest brown bear population, some 20 individuals.

SVALBARD

The islands of **Svalbard**, the northernmost part of Norway, lie between 74°–81°N, far above the Arctic Circle. Some 2,700 people make Svalbard their permanent home, mostly working in mining or at the various research centres. Spitsbergen is the largest island in the group, with Longyearbyen the capital and largest town. Longyearbyen can be reached by plane from Oslo or Tromsø, and Svalbard is included on some Arctic cruise itineraries. Tourism in Svalbard is a fairly recent activity, but since the late 1980s it has been steadily on the increase. It is not a destination geared towards independent or spontaneous travel, nor is it light on the pocket, but it is a

Giant crab

The red king crab, *Paralithodes camtschaticus*, is an unusually large crab species found in the Barents Sea in the far north of Norway. Their leg span can reach as much as 1.8 metres (6ft).

once-in-a-lifetime experience. The season is short for those who would like to experience the Arctic summer and it is recommended that accommodation and all tours and activities are booked well in advance for June to August.

One of the main reasons independent ventures into Svalbard are somewhat discouraged is the presence of polar bears, a protected species across the islands. There are around 3,000 in Svalbard: in other words, a few more than there are people. Visitors are advised to take organised tours and to be very cautious if they come into contact with a bear.

SIGHTS AND ACTIVITIES

The activities offered in Svalbard vary depending on the time of year you choose to visit, but some sights can be experienced year-round. In **Longyearbyen** there is the **Svalbard Museum** (www.svalbardmuseum.no; Feb–Sept 10am–5pm, Oct–Jan noon–5pm) in Svalbardporten, with exhibitions covering Svalbard's 400-year history from whaling and trapping to mining. **Galleri Svalbard** is located in the Nybyen part of town and has artworks by local artists depicting Svalbard motifs. The **Spitsbergen Airship Museum** (www.spitsbergenairship museum.com; daily 9am–5pm) charts the history of the three airships that have tried to reach the North Pole from Svalbard. From June to October it's possible to take boat trips around the islands in large vessels or in smaller rubber dinghies that get closer to the coastline and the birdlife. You could also go hiking, kayaking, glacier hiking, fossil hunting or exploring the flora and fauna of the islands, all with experienced guides.

From November to May there is dog-sledding, skiing, ice caving, snowshoeing and snowmobile safaris, among other activities. In some parts of the islands these winter activities are offered all year round, as 63 percent of Svalbard is covered by glaciers and the snow never goes away. Bear in mind that this is an Arctic wilderness and a fragile environment. Svalbard tourism council has more information and guidelines for visitors, as well as a handy list of tour operators for all the activities on offer (tel: 79-02 55 50; www.visitsvalbard.com; Svalbard Reiseliv, Longyearbyen).

JAN MAYEN

This volcanic island, lying between Greenland and Norway, is the country's furthest outpost. There are no commercial flights and no natural harbours. To visit you need to obtain a permit from the Norwegian government. Independent travel is not possible but an organisation called EcoExpeditions arranges trips by sailing boat (www.ecoexpeditions.no).

An old steam train, once used to transport coal from mines in Svalbard

Norway is a hiker's paradise

WHAT TO DO

Norway, although mainly known for its natural wonders, also has a rich and varied history and cultural life. In summer there are many events that combine nature and culture, with festivals and concerts held outdoors in scenic settings. Winter offers an increasing range of options from first-rate skiing and other winter sports, to Christmas markets and the spectacular phenomenon of the Northern Lights.

SPORTS AND OUTDOOR PURSUITS

SUMMER

Hiking and glacier walking. Nothing is a more popular Norwegian pastime than to *'gå på tur'* – something that involves strapping on a good pair of boots, taking a packed lunch and spending a day hiking amid some of the glorious scenery, be it mountain, fjord, forest or field. There are countless hiking trails, and good-quality maps can usually be obtained from local tourist offices. Some of Norway's many national parks – 37 on the mainland, seven on Svalbard – such as Jotunheimen or Hardangervidda are good bets, and the majority of trails are well kept and clearly marked with cairns or signposts. If you are planning to hike, bear in mind that the season only runs from May to October and in the far north it's even shorter. The weather can be very changeable even in the height of summer, so take local advice before setting out. The Norwegian Trekking Association has further information and organises tours (www.dnt.no). The short summer season is also a good time to try out glacier walking. Nigardsbreen, an arm of Jostedalsbreen glacier, allows the adventurous to explore the glacier, with an experienced guide, on two- to five-hour blue ice walks, from mid-June to the middle of September (www.jostedal. com). Glacier walking on Okstindan and Svartisen in the Arctic Circle can also be arranged with Rana SpesialSport (tel: 911-48 455; email: egil@spesialsport.no).

Cycling. Norwegian roads are comparatively quiet, making them excellent for cycling in spring, summer and autumn. City roads tend to have cycle paths and in the countryside traffic is rarely a problem. It's easy to rent bikes, even in rural areas, where hotels and guesthouses often rent them out by the hour or by the day. In mountainous areas cycling can be challenging and also bear in mind that distances can be great, with facilities few and far between, especially in the far north. The Navvies' Road (Rallarvegen) is one of the most popular routes, running from Haugastøl or Finse, to Flåm or Voss, 108km (67 miles) at its longest. Another popular option is the North Sea Cycle Route, part

---

☉ GÅ PÅ TUR: MASTERING THE GREAT OUTDOORS

To *gå på tur*, literally to 'go on tour', is one of those quintessentially Norwegian concepts that seemingly every Norwegian will indulge in, if not every weekend, then certainly on a regular basis. It involves heading out into the countryside, in warm clothes and sturdy footwear, and hiking through the great outdoors – often in the mountains, but any bit of countryside will do. The day is not complete without the obligatory stop to eat a packed lunch, usually doorstep sandwiches and a thermos of hot, black coffee. On summer weekends, in the many scenic areas of the country, whole families, young and old, venture forth and energetically conquer the peaks and fjordlands from north to south, particularly in the 33 national parks.

of the world's longest biking route, passing through seven countries. Bike Norway can give you further information and supply route maps (www.cycling norway.no).

Fishing. In a country blessed with so much water, it is no surprise that fishing is ever-popular. It is possible to go deep-sea fishing, freshwater fishing or salmon fishing. The Lofoten Islands have some of the best waters and arguably

A rural bike ride at Oslofjord

the most authentic fishing culture, with their old fishermen's cabins, *rorbuer*, many of which offer accommodation. There are organised fishing tours in many parts of Norway (check with local tourist offices) or you can get a national fishing licence, available to purchase online from www.inatur.no.

Climbing. Mountaineering is a popular sport in many areas. Lofoten, with its stark, forbidding mountains, is a centre for rock climbing, with a climbing school in Henningsvær (www.nordnorsk klatreskole.no). Other areas include Jotunheimen, where the peaks reach 2,000 metres (over 6,000ft), Vesterålen Mountains and the Lyngen Alps. You could also try ice climbing – climbing up frozen waterfalls – in Rjukan. The Norwegian Trekking Association, DNT, runs mountain-climbing courses (www.dnt.no).

Rafting, sailing and canoeing. Rafting can be done both on the many rivers and at sea. Deep-sea rafting on the Vestfjord between the Lofoten Islands and the mainland is possible if

The midnight sun is best viewed at sea

the wind and currents are right. Sailing is popular mainly in southern Norway and on the Oslo fjord. Canoeing and kayaking can be tried pretty much any-where there is water, but the western fjords are par-ticularly scenic, while the far north is more tranquil, with fewer pleasure boats and ferries. The Norwegian Canoe Association has more information (www.padling.no).

Wildlife and birdwatching. There are ample opportunities to spot wildlife such as reindeer and elk in many parts of Norway, or the more illusive musk oxen in Dovrefjell National Park (www.moskussafari.no), and the giant king crab in Finnmark. Birdlife is abundant with 473 recorded species, inland and along the coastline. For a com-bination of birdwatching and king crab safaris, Arctic Tourist (www.arctictourist.no) in Finnmark is a good option.

Midnight sun. The midnight sun is visible in many parts of north-ern Norway from May to August depending on latitude. The best and most unrestricted views are from higher ground or at sea.

WINTER

Cross-country and downhill skiing. Skiing is the most popu-lar winter sport in Norway with more than 7,000km (4,350 miles) of cross-country tracks laid out by the DNT (Norwegian Trekking Association) alone. There are even tracks within the Oslo city limits and most municipalities have their own ski tracks, sometimes floodlit in the evenings for after-work exercise. Jotunheimen, Rondane and Dovrefjell national parks have some of the best cross-country skiing in Norway. Alpine or downhill skiing is also an option in various parts of the country, from Geilo, Hemsedal and Trysil in the centre, to Narvik further north. The best time for skiing is February to April, but it's usually possible to ski from November until mid-May. For good up-to-date information on snow conditions, check www.skiinfo.no.

Dog-sledding. There are organised dog-sledding trips, mostly in the north of the country, that last for anything from an hour or two up to five-day excursions. You can choose between steering your own sled or sitting snugly wrapped up with your own musher and a team of dogs doing all the hard work. Visit

Sailing is a popular pastime in Norway

Ice-fishing is a fun, if chilly, activity

Norway has more information (www.visitnorway.com); or try
Nordland Adventures (www.nordlandturselskap.no).

Ice-skating. Come winter a number of outdoor ice rinks
open up, such as the popular one in Oslo city centre, near
the National Theatre. Then there are the natural ice rinks in
the form of frozen lakes, rivers and fjords – but do take local
advice before venturing out on these. At the man-made ice
rinks, skates can usually be hired and it's sometimes possible
to have lessons.

Ice-fishing or *pimpling*. For this sport a hole is simply drilled
through the ice, which you can then fish through and get a good
catch, even in winter. Bring waterproof gloves and a thermos of
hot chocolate. A company called Competent Travels organises
three-day ice-fishing safaris from Tromsø.

Northern Lights. The Northern Lights, *aurora borealis*, can
best be spotted in October, February and March, between 6pm

and 1am at night. The best displays of light can be seen above the Arctic Circle, where there is less light pollution, but the Northern Lights can also be seen further south. Remember to wrap up warm on these excursions.

SHOPPING

Prices can be high for consumer goods, but over 4,000 shops across Norway are participating in a tax-free shopping scheme. Look for the tax-free logo in the windows of participating shops. The sales tax/VAT in Norway is 25 percent on many items (15 percent for food) and 12–19 percent can be claimed back by visitors from non-EU/EEA countries. The refund can be made through the Global Refund Cash Refund Offices at land border crossings, airports, on board ferries and cruise ships.

The quality of most items is usually very high and some of the handicraft traditions go back hundreds of years. Look for the *salg* sign in windows, indicating a sale or special offers.

WHERE TO SHOP

The main cities of Oslo, Bergen, Stavanger and Trondheim all have good shopping areas, and some of Norway's smaller towns also have interesting shops, particularly for handicrafts. Oslo has everything from department stores such as Glasmagasinet and House of Oslo, Norway's largest, to quirky, independent boutiques in the up-and-coming area of Grünerløkka and trendy Majorstuen. Aker Brygge is another good shopping area, where the old converted shipyard in the harbour houses shops, restaurants and bars. In Bergen, the area around Bryggen, Strandkaien, Strandgaten and Torget has many small, interesting shops whose goods include handicrafts, furs and knitwear. This is also the area of the famous Fish Market, perfect for buying lunch, fresh fish and seafood.

The Stavanger region is particularly good for glass, and you can visit glass-blowing studios and buy the products in speciality craft shops. The centre of Trondheim, Midtbyen, has both traditional and modern shopping opportunities: the Trondheim Torg mall, near the main square, has 75 stores, plus cafés and restaurants, while more old-fashioned shops can be found in Jomfrugaten (Maiden Street), where most of the businesses are run by women. There are plenty of other shopping options in Norway. Tromsø, for example, has numerous shops and boutiques housed in old, wooden buildings; and in the far north there are excellent Sami handicrafts (called *duodji*), such as silverware and items made from reindeer hide or bone.

WHAT TO BUY

This is just a small selection of recommended things to buy that are either unique to Norway or particularly good value.

Handicrafts. The craft traditions in Norway go back many hundred years and the roots of today's modern designs, using locally available materials, can be found in the old crafts. Knitwear, such as sweaters, scarves, gloves, mittens and hats, is internationally renowned, as it is of excellent quality. Woodcraft, glassware, silverware and jewellery, reindeer pelts and weavings are other popular items to take home. In the far north, as mentioned above, there are interesting Sami handicrafts for sale.

Local food and drink. Norway has a number of locally produced specialities, ranging from smoked salmon and stockfish (*tørrfisk*) to akvavit, and Mack beer from the world's northernmost brewery in Tromsø. Reindeer and elk salamis and cloudberry jams are other products to take home if you want to relive a taste of Norway.

Clothes. Men's and women's clothes are often nicely designed, but can be expensive. Knitwear features heavily, but there are also plenty of lighter items and summer clothing. As a rule there are more individual shops than chains, although international brands are quite common in the main cities. Norwegian designer shop Moods of Norway has made it big in Japan and Beverly Hills with its colourful designs (www.moodsofnorway.com).

Sports and outdoor gear. Norwegians are quite possibly the sportiest people in the world and this is reflected in their shops. Excellent all-weather outdoor gear and winter clothes

Fresh produce at Bergen fish market

can be found across the country, including entire ski outfits, as well as skis and ice-skates.

ENTERTAINMENT

In a country as large as Norway, with a population of slightly more than five million, the quality and variety of entertainment varies widely from region to region and, of course, between city and countryside. There is a long-standing musical and theatrical tradition in Norway, with a number of festivals celebrating both these art forms, particularly during the summer months. Tickets for events in Norway can be booked in advance via the Norwegian branch of Ticketmaster (tel: 81-53 31 33; www.ticketmaster.no). Tourist offices are sometimes able to help out with booking events and concerts.

MUSIC, OPERA AND DANCE

Classical music is alive and well in Norway, celebrating national composers such as Edvard Grieg. The **Oslo Philharmonic Orchestra** has an excellent reputation, and its home base is at the city's **Konserthus**; the season starts at the end of August and runs until early June (check https://ofo.no for concert

All that jazz in Norway

Oslo's iconic Opera House

schedules and tickets). **Bergen Philharmonic Orchestra** is based at **Grieghallen** (www.harmonien.no); and there is also the **Norwegian Arctic Philharmonic Orchestra** based in Tromsø (www.noso.no).

Jazz is very big in Norway (see Calendar of Events, page 95), and while the classical music season runs from autumn to spring, jazz festivals and venues kick off in summer. There are well over 30 jazz venues across the country, including some that are off the beaten track. For more information see www.jazz-clubs-worldwide.com. In recent years there has been a rise in so-called Black Metal rock music and this genre is one of Norway's greatest musical exports. Traditional Norwegian folk music remains popular, in particular the Halling folk dance and fiddle-playing, as used by Alexander Rybak, winner of the 2009 Eurovision Song Contest. The dance hails from Hallingdal valley, in the Buskerud district.

Oslo's **Opera House** is home to the national opera and the national ballet (www.operaen.no for programme information). In a stunning building with excellent acoustics, it has an extensive programme of international operas, concerts and ballets, as well as a festival of chamber music every August.

THEATRE AND CINEMA

Norway has a proud theatrical tradition, dating back to the late 19th-century works of **Henrik Ibsen** and **Bjørnstjerne Bjørnson**. The **National Theatre** in Oslo (www.nationaltheatret. no), **Den Nationale Scene** in Bergen (www.dns.no), **Rogaland Teater** in Stavanger (www.rogaland-teater.no) and **Trøndelag Teater** in Trondheim (www.trondelag-teater.no) all have extensive programmes, but, naturally, most plays and shows tend to be in Norwegian. At the cinema, on the other hand, films are almost exclusively shown in their original language, with Norwegian subtitles.

NIGHTLIFE

The cities of **Oslo, Bergen**, **Stavanger** and **Trondheim** all have a busy nightlife, with bars and clubs often staying open until the small hours all year round. In summer, areas such as **Aker Brygge** in Oslo are packed with people enjoying alfresco meals and drinks in the evening. Bars usually shut around 1am or later at the weekend. Bear in mind that the very high cost of alcohol can make a night out expensive, but some places have a happy hour for after-work or early-evening drinks.

Adults only

For entry to nightclubs the minimum age can be fairly high, often 21 or above, so remember to bring ID if look younger than you are.

Amusement parks are bound to keep little ones happy

In rural areas nightlife is a lot more limited in scope, but there is usually at least one local bar, which can be an interesting experience to visit, since this is where local people congregate. Many of the smaller **fjord communities** are busy in summer and hotels or guesthouses often have bars that are open to the public, as well as to guests. Similarly, **ski resorts** tend to have a good nightlife in winter. The Oslo tourist board at www.visitoslo.com has a useful 'What's on in Oslo' guide.

ACTIVITIES FOR CHILDREN

Norway is a very child-friendly nation. Public transport not only has pram access, but buses have special seats that convert to child seats for longer journeys. Most restaurants and cafés have highchairs and offer children's menus. It is not unusual for hotels, campsites and other accommodation to have play areas for little ones and sometimes children's pools. Towns and municipalities have outdoor playgrounds and many public facilities have dedicated play areas. Children often get substantial discounts on entry fees to sights, at ski centres and on public transport. For many attractions there are also family tickets available.

Cities aren't always the best places for children, but Oslo has numerous ways to keep them entertained and occupied, such as the many museums with interactive areas (www.visitoslo.com). Just 20km (12.5 miles) outside Oslo lies **TusenFryd Amusement Park** (late Apr–early Oct, times vary), with lots of rides, including Europe's first 5D attraction and a water park. Fifteen km (9 miles) north of Lillehammer, **Hunderfossen Family Park** (www.hunderfossen.no; times vary) has some 50 attractions including a troll park, a high rope course, rafting and a full-scale fairy-tale palace. In winter months it turns into a Winter Park. **Bø Sommarland** (www.sommarland.no; June–Aug), in Telemark, 80km (50 miles) west of Oslo, is Scandinavia's largest water park, with 20 different pools and slides. They also have a Tarzan track, clown shows, canoeing and Europe's only water roller-coaster, the Master Blaster, among other attractions. **Kristiansand Zoo**, just outside Kristiansand, is open year-round, with wildlife from all over the world in five separate parks, including a Children's Farm and an area where you can explore the Nordic wilderness. The zoo also has pirate ships and a games area (www.dyreparken.no).

Rockheim in Trondheim (www.rockheim.no; Tue–Wed and Fri 10am–4pm, Thu until 8pm, Sat–Sun until 5pm) is the national interactive experience centre for all things related to Norwegian rock and pop. It's an excellent place to drop off your grumpy teenagers for the afternoon.

Sporting activities are also very child-friendly, and it's usually possible to rent sports equipment such as skis and ice-skates for children, even for toddlers. Norwegian children start skiing, skating and joining their parents for hikes from a very young age and there are good sports instructors for youngsters of all ages.

CALENDAR OF EVENTS

January Northern Lights Festival (Tromsø).

February Opera Festival (Kristiansund).

March Holmenkollen Ski Festival (Oslo). The Winter Festival (Narvik), includes sports events, concerts and carnival. The Birkebeiner Race (Rena to Lillehammer), a 53km (33-mile) cross-country ski race, with up to 12,000 participants.

April Jazz festival (Voss), three days of jazz and folk.

May International Festival (Bergen), one of the largest musical events in Scandinavia.

June American emigration festival (Stavanger and Kvinesdal), commemorating the many Norwegians who emigrated to North America. Midsummer (nationwide), celebrating the summer solstice. Midnight Sun Marathon (Tromsø), the northern Norway marathon that starts at midnight.

July International Jazz Festival (Kongsberg), international jazz artists and open-air concerts held in many venues around town. Bislett Games (Oslo), international athletics competition. International Jazz Festival (Molde), the oldest jazz festival in Norway, held over six days. Olsok festival (Trondheim), commemorating St Olaf the Holy; and the Oi food festival (Trondheim). Gladmat festival (Stavanger), celebrating all things foodie.

August Telemark International Folk Music Festival (Bø), folk music and folk dance festival. Peer Gynt Festival (Vinstra), events in honour of Ibsen's fictional character. Jazz Festival (Oslo), which has been running since 1986. Chamber Music Festival (Oslo), chamber music performed at Akershus Castle and Fortress.

September Oslo Marathon (Oslo).

December Christmas markets (Oslo and nationwide). From Advent (beginning of December) onwards at weekends in many parts of Norway, markets sell unusual Christmas gifts, handicrafts and local delicacies. Nobel Peace Prize Ceremony (Oslo), held at Oslo City Hall, 10 December annually.

 # EATING OUT

Norwegian cuisine has come into its own in recent years with an emphasis on fresh local produce, and the country's fish and seafood are world-famous, from *bacalao* to Arctic prawns and smoked salmon. There is plenty for the adventurous carnivore to sample as well, with reindeer and elk increasingly featuring on many of the best restaurant menus. A new generation of chefs is rediscovering local produce, sometimes sticking solely to traditional recipes, sometimes adding more international flavours.

☉ FOOD FESTIVALS

Norwegians take their food seriously and over the last decade a number of food festivals have sprung up across the country. *Norsk Matglede* in Geilo, *Gladmat* in Stavanger, the Norwegian Food Festival in Ålesund and *Oi Trøndersk Matfesival* in Trondheim, are just some of the events celebrating all things foodie in Norway. Programmes include everything from tasting sessions to cooking lessons, master chefs' workshops, lectures and special offers from local restaurateurs. Most keep the focus firmly Norwegian, looking into the history and traditions behind modern-day national cuisine, but *Gladmat*, taking over the scenic harbour area of Stavanger every summer, has a more international feel to it. Geilo, at the other end of the spectrum, emphasises small-scale producers and organic food. The festivals are often held in the height of summer, with stalls set up for outdoor sampling and alfresco eating, in some of Norway's loveliest settings.

Rustic Norwegian home-cooking was traditionally based around what produce was available locally, depending on the changing seasons. Many dishes popular to this day have their roots in the farming or fishing communities from days gone by and there is a strong emphasis on fish or game, in the coastal and inland areas respectively. The topography of Norway – coast, farmland, forest, highland and mountains –

Café culture in Oslo

has meant that different ingredients are popular in different parts of the country. Pickled, dried, smoked, salted and fermented foods all have their origins in the days before refrigeration, preservatives and modern cooking methods, when it was necessary to find alternative ways for storing and preparing foodstuffs that needed to last through the long winters. Some dishes, both fish and meat, have strong flavours and can be a bit of an acquired taste for the uninitiated, but for the most part Norwegian cuisine is fresh, wholesome and tasty, and portions are generous.

This is not to say that you will only find Norwegian food – the cuisine here is increasingly international in flavour. Pizza, pasta and burgers are as common as *lefse*, a round flatbread, traditionally made of potato, and *sursild*, pickled herring. A number of international cuisines such as Italian, Chinese, Thai and Indian are well represented, at least in the bigger cities. Also in recent years, a number of annual food festivals, featuring both Norwegian and

Fish and seafood can be found on most menus

international cuisine, take place during the summer. Food culture in Norway has numerous regional variations, and what is consumed in Oslo can differ substantially from what is popular in, for example, Bergen or Tromsø, but generally speaking there is an emphasis on using local produce whenever possible. As a rule, in the countryside many of the best restaurants can be found in hotels and guesthouses, which usually serve food to non-guests as well as to residents.

WHEN TO EAT

People tend to eat comparatively early in Norway. Despite the majority of Norwegians working away from the home, dinner is still consumed surprisingly early, perhaps harking back to a different era. It is not unusual for restaurants to start serving dinner from 5pm, and in smaller towns it can be difficult to get a meal after 9 or 10pm, when all but a few bars will be closing.

WHAT TO EAT

Most hotels serve an international-style breakfast, but for Norwegians breakfast can be anything from hail and hearty to a quick cup of coffee, always taken black. For the working Norwegian the packed lunch, *matpakke*, still reigns supreme, even though eating out or buying a sandwich is becoming more common.

As you would expect, Norwegians eat more fish than people in many other countries, and fish has been a staple of their diet for many centuries. Seafood, on the other hand, is more of a recent addition to the diet.

There are more than 200 species of fish and shellfish in Norwegian waters, some wild, some farmed. Norway is one of the world's largest exporters, sending around 3 million tonnes of its sea harvest to consumers abroad. Some of the most common fish to be found on menus and in markets are cod, salmon, trout, herring, Arctic char, pollack, monkfish, mackerel and redfish. And as if that wasn't enough variety, there is also plaice, turbot, coley, ling, tusk, whiting, haddock, catfish, halibut and flounder to choose from – and these are just the most common species.

Fish is prepared in all sorts of ways, but Norwegian cooking is quite light on spices and seasoning – salt, pepper and a few different herbs, such as dill or mustard seeds, are most

⊙ SAMI COOKING

Traditional Sami cooking, much like Norwegian cooking in general, was based around what was available and what the land could yield at different times of year. However, many Sami were in the past largely self-sufficient and lived on the fish or meat they themselves could catch. Although much has changed in terms of Sami lifestyle over the last century, many of the staples in Sami cooking have remained. Arctic char is still one of the best-loved fish, and reindeer still forms part of the diet. All parts of the animal, from marrow to blood, are used. *Renkok*, or reindeer stew, is still a popular dish and black pudding is made with reindeer blood and flour. Reindeer also used to be milked, and dairy products such as cheese were produced.

frequently used. Boiling, braising, poaching, smoking and pickling are popular ways of preparing fish, often served simply with boiled new potatoes and a bit of butter. Best known of all is probably the Norwegian salmon dish known as *gravlaks*, literally meaning 'buried salmon', a form of curing the fish with salt and sugar. Fish soups, usually milk-based, feature heavily along Norway's coastline, containing a variety of fish and seafood, as well as vegetables and potatoes. Herrings, pickled with all sorts of tasty additions from mustard and onion to tomato and herbs, are another trusty favourite. Fermented trout, *rakfisk*, is a dish that is something of an acquired taste, along with *lutefisk*, dried and salted ling or cod, steeped in lye. It is traditionally eaten at Christmas time and has a very distinctive taste and aroma – or some would say stench. *Tørrfisk*, or stockfish, is a tremendously popular snack eaten either dry or cooked.

Something else found on many menus along the coast, particularly in the north, might raise a few eyebrows: whale meat. Norwegians, on the whole, don't find it controversial to eat whale, and the history of whaling goes back a long time in the north of the country. Whale steak, whale burgers and the like are found in many restaurants, although less so now since the whale hunting quota has been cut.

Shellfish, although only commonly eaten since the latter part of the 20th century, has taken off in a big way and Norwegians are now great consumers of seafood, including the Arctic prawn, lobsters, oysters,

Christmas flavours

Christmas is the time to try lutefish, mutton rib, ptarmigan and of course beverages of the alcoholic kind – *gløgg* (similar to mulled wine, often spiked with a stronger spirit), *julaøl* (Christmas beer) and, strongest of all, akvavit.

Presentation can be nearly as important as taste

mussels, scallops and crabs. The enormous red king crab, caught near the North Cape, is particularly good. In summer, crab parties, *krabbelag*, are held where the crabs are eaten just with rustic bread, butter and perhaps a lemon wedge.

But it is not all fish and seafood in Norway – there are also plenty of meat dishes, and dairy products are ever-popular. For the carnivore, Norway has a lot to offer the adventurous. There are reindeer dishes in the north, and elk, including *gravet elg*, a sugar- and salt-cured elk dish, using the same procedure as for *gravlaks*. Pork, beef, chicken, lamb and mutton are also widely used. Meatballs, *kjøttekaker*, are popular, often with a tart lingonberry sauce or relish. Mutton stew with cabbage, *fårikål* (literally 'mutton in cabbage'), is a warming winter dish, served with potatoes. Sausages of all kinds, including reindeer and elk salamis, or the simple hot dogs, *varme pølser*, are often sold as snacks from

Fresh berries form the basis of many Norwegian desserts

kiosks or stalls. In many restaurants dishes still retain a seasonal quality, with good fresh berries in summer and early autumn for the desserts, sauces or marinades, followed by a wide variety of mushroom dishes slightly later in the year, excellent game in autumn and hearty stews, soups and casseroles in winter.

Vegetables do not figure prominently on menus, however, and this can make finding good options a bit tricky for vegetarian visitors, and particularly for vegans, but even this is beginning to change, at least in the bigger cities.

Bread accompanies many meals, and it is usually of the whole grain variety, and a sandwich in Norway tends to be the open kind – just one slice of bread, piled high with all kinds of goodies.

Desserts tend to focus on fresh berries, with cream or ice cream, and waffles are a Norwegian institution, served with clotted cream and a variety of berry jams to choose from – strawberries, cloudberries, raspberries and blueberries being the most popular options.

WHAT TO DRINK

Norwegians love their coffee: in fact they are the world's second largest per-capita consumer, downing some 160 litres

(35 gallons) per person per year. Having a coffee break, meeting friends and family for coffee and cake, or just having a large mug of coffee at any time of day, could all be considered Norwegian pastimes. There is even an alcoholic kind of coffee, known as *karsk*, which originated in Trøndelag. This usually has a dash of vodka or, more often than not, moonshine spirit, added to it.

Tea has become more common in recent years and there is usually a decent selection of teas available in shops, hotels and restaurants. Soft drinks and fruit juices, either national or international brands, are widely available and popular. Also, in rural areas, many people still prefer to drink a large glass of milk with their meal.

Norway is well known internationally for its strict alcohol policy, but despite this, Norwegians do like to drink. The state-run monopoly, *Vinmonopolet*, is the only kind of shop licensed to sell alcohol for home consumption, and even though prices can be quite expensive, due to the high taxes, they are far more reasonable than the prices for alcoholic drinks bought in bars and restaurants.

Norway has long been a beer-drinking nation and there are various national brews, such as Ringnes from Oslo, Hansa from Bergen, CB from Kristiansand, and Mack, from the world's northernmost brewery, based in Tromsø. Norway also makes distilled spirits of the stronger kind; akvavit (*akevitt*) and vodka. Vikingfjord is Norway's own brand of premium vodka. Akvavits such as Gammel Opland, Linie and Gilde are well-known

Strong tastes

Norwegians like their coffee black – no milk, no sugar, and a very large mug. And it hasn't made them a nation of insomniacs.

A selection of Norwegian craft beers

Norwegian brands, and the tradition of drinking akvavit is mostly associated with Christmas. The rest of the year other, more international, spirits are consumed. Wine is becoming more popular, but it remains comparatively expensive. In fact, drinking wine with your meal in a restaurant can sometimes more than double your bill. It is fairly common, especially in rural areas, to encounter moonshine – *hjemmebrent* – a strong spirit, usually potato-based.

TO HELP YOU ORDER

Restaurant **restaurant**
A table for..., please **et bord til..., takk**
I'd like a/an/some... **Jeg vil gjerne ha en/ett/noen...**
I don't eat meat/I'm a vegetarian **Jeg spiser ikke kjøtt/
    Jeg er vegetarianer**
Could I have the bill, please? **Kan jeg få regningen, takk?**

beer **øl**
bread **brød**
breakfast **frokost**
butter **smør**
coffee **kaffe**
cream **fløte**
dessert **dessert**
dinner **middag**
fish **fisk**
lunch **lunsj**
main course **hovedrett**
meat **kjøtt**
milk **melk**

pepper **pepper**
potatoes **poteter**
red/white wine **rød/hvitvin**
salad **salat**
salt **salt**
sandwich **smørebrød/ sandwich**
soup **suppe**
starter **forrett**
sugar **sukker**
vegetables **grønnsaker**
water **vann**

MENU READER

blåbær blueberries
blåskjell mussels
bringebær raspberries
dyrekjøtt venison
egg egg
elg elk/moose
fårikål mutton stew
fiskesuppe fish soup
geitost goat's cheese
gravlaks salt and sugar cured salmon
hummer lobster
is ice cream
jordbær strawberries
kake cake
klippfisk salted and dried stockfish

kjøttkaker meatballs
krabbe crab
kylling chicken
lefse flatbread made from potato
multer cloudberries
oksekjøtt beef
pølser sausages
rein reindeer
reker shrimp/prawn
sauekjøtt mutton
skalldyr seafood
sopp mushrooms
svinekjøtt pork
sursild pickled herring
torsk cod
tyttebær lingonberries

PLACES TO EAT

We have used the following symbols to give an idea of the price for a three-course meal for one, not including alcohol:

$$$ over NOK700
$$ NOK300–700
$ below NOK300

OSLO

The area of **Aker Brygge**, on the harbour front, has a wide variety of restaurants that are popular year-round, but it is particularly buzzing in summer, when many of the 40-odd establishments have outdoor seating. See www.akerbrygge.no for a full list of restaurants and bars. Another good area for food, particularly at lunchtime, is along **Karl Johans Gate**, the main street, running through the centre.

De Fem Stuer $$$ *Kongeveien 26, tel: 22-92 20 00*, www.scandic hotels.com. A top-class international restaurant housed within Holmenkollen Park Hotel, a 100-year old building near the Holmenkollen ski centre.

Eataly $–$$ *Bryggetorget 18, tel: 22-83 13 00*, www.eataly.no. Good-quality Italian restaurant. Large, gorgeous pizzas and pasta dishes; children's portions, and wine by the glass. Lovely outdoor seating, overlooking Aker Brygge and Tjuvholmen, and a central fireplace for winter days. The outdoor seats have sheepskins to sit on and blankets to wrap up in, should it get chilly.

Frognerseteren Restaurant and Café $–$$$ *Holmenkollveien 200, tel: 22-92 40 40*, www.frognerseteren.no. Café Seterstua and Restaurant Finstua are both located in this historic building on the way to Holmenkollen ski jump, overlooking Oslo. Finstua serves first-rate Norwegian cuisine for lunch and dinner; Café Seterstua, which opens at 11am, is more casual. Frognerseteren is very popular with local people, and is reached by tram from central Oslo.

Kaffistova $ *Rosenkrantz gate 8, tel: 23-21 41 00,* www.kaffistova.com. This café-diner in the Hotel Bondeheimen serves hearty, wholesome Norwegian home-cooking at reasonable prices.

Maaemo $$$ *Schweigardsgate 15B, tel: 22-17 99 69,* www.maaemo. no. The dishes at this seriously upmarket restaurant are made with organic and foraged ingredients. Innovative contemporary Nordic cuisine with prices to match.

Solsiden $$$ *Søndre Akershus kai 34, tel: 22-33 36 30,* www.solsiden. no. One of the best fish and seafood restaurants in Oslo, this converted warehouse right on the waterfront is open May–mid-September only, but remains ever-popular.

Theatercafeen $$$ *Stortingsgata 24-26, tel: 22-82 40 50,* www.theater cafeen.no. This legendary Viennese-style café has been popular with diners for over 100 years. The place to eat and to be seen, good for celebrity-spotting – and the food is excellent too.

THE SOUTH AND SOUTHEASTERN BORDERLANDS

Fredriksten Kro $$ *Fredriksten Fortress (Festning) Halden, tel: 69-17 52 32.* Traditional inn near the fortress overlooking Halden. Serves 53 different types of sandwiches and there is a special cake menu.

Sjøhuset Restaurant $$ *Østre Strandgate 12A Kristiansand, tel: 38-02 62 60.* Excellent seafood restaurant housed in a former salt storage warehouse. There's a special summer menu, seasonal fare, and good fish and chips.

Tollboden Café & Restaurant $$–$$$ *P.A. Heuchsgate 4, Kragerø, tel: 35-98 90 90.* Converted 19th-century ship's cabin that serves Italian, French and Nordic-inspired cuisine. It also has a special menu for dogs.

STAVANGER

Amy's Coffeebar $ *Norwegian Petroleum Museum, Kjeringholmen, tel: 51-86 07 65*. A cosy coffeehouse right in the city centre with outdoor tables, a warm atmosphere and, of course, great coffee and cakes.

Bølgen & Moi Stavanger $$–$$$ *Norwegian Petroleum Museum, Kjeringholmen, tel: 51-93 93 51*, www.bolgenogmoi.no. Popular brasserie (with several branches elsewhere in Norway), located inside one of Stavanger's most unusual museums.

Sjøhuset Skagen $$$ *Skagenkaien 16, tel: 51-89 51 80*. Good-quality Norwegian and international food is on the menu in a historic building dating from the 18th century.

BERGEN AND AROUND

Altona Vinbar $$ *Strandgaten 81, Bergen, tel: 55-30 40 00*. In an historic wine cellar, this is Bergen's oldest tavern, which also serves good food. It's dark, cosy and intimate, perfect for romantic dinners. The seafood is particularly good, as, of course, is the wine list.

Bergen Fish Market $ *Fisketorget, Bergen, tel: 55-55 20 00 (near the tourist information office)*. Bergen fish market, teeming with stalls selling all kinds of fish and seafood, is an attraction and an experience in itself. You can pick up excellent lunchtime snacks, fresh from the sea – anything from smoked salmon baguettes to huge seafood trays, to be enjoyed on the spot or as a takeaway. Some of the stalls have wooden benches for seating.

Bryggeloftet & Stuene $$ *Bryggen 11, Bergen, tel: 55-30 20 70*, www.bryggeloftet.no. Situated in historic Bryggen, a Unesco World Heritage Site, this place has been run by the same family for generations, and offers Norwegian cooking at its finest. There are traditional 'lutefisk parties', game dishes, and there are lovely views over the fish market.

Fløien Folkerestaurant $$–$$$ *Fløyfjellet 2, Bergen, tel: 55-33 69 99*, www.bellevue.no. Originally opened in 1925, this restaurant at the top of Mount Fløyen, reached by the Fløibanen funicular, has Bergen's most spectacular views and offers innovative Norwegian cooking. Well worth the trip.

Ringheim Kafe $–$$ *Vangsgata 34, Voss, tel: 56-51 13 65*. Old-fashioned café with good lunchtime meals at reasonable prices.

CENTRAL NORWAY AND THE WESTERN FJORDS

Gamletorvet Spiseri $$–$$$ *Øvre Torvgate 24, Gjøvik, tel: 61-17 04 44*. Housed in the old working men's club, this rustic restaurant serves contemporary and traditional Norwegian dishes and is part of the Historical Hotels and Restaurants of Norway.

Hallingstuene $$$ *Geilovegen 56, opposite the railway station, Geilo, tel: 32-09 12 50, www.hallingstuene.no*. This cosy restaurant, complete with open fires and traditional paintings, is run by a Norwegian celebrity chef and his wife. Specialities include ptarmigan and game dishes, as well as 'Halling tapas' using produce from the area.

Hardanger Saft-og Siderfabrikk, Lekve Gardsrestaurant $–$$ *Lekve Gard, Ulvik, tel: 901-22 835*. Local gourmet food in lovely setting, in a cider factory. The restaurant is open in summer only; advance booking essential. There is also a café with snacks and cider tastings.

Hummer & Kanari $$–$$$ *Kongensgate 19, Ålesund, tel: 70-12 80 08*. Restaurant and bistro serving modern European food with an Italian twist. Good pasta and seafood.

TRØNDELAG AND NORDLAND

Bacalao $–$$ *Kirkegata 23, Svolvær, Lofoten Islands, tel: 76-07 94 00*. Nice bistro with soups, sandwiches and salads, in a harbour setting. Terrace seating and a fireplace for when it gets chilly.

Le Bistro $$ *Munkegata 25, Trondheim, tel: 73-60 60 24*. Stylish restaurant, with changing daytime and evening menus, serving French favourites, such as crocque monsieur, entrecôte and crème brûlée, alongside Norwegian seafood.

Bjørk $$ *Storgata 8, 2nd floor, Bodø, tel: 75-52 40 40,* www.restaurant bjork.no. Café, bar and restaurant with balcony seating in summer, inside Glasmagasinet, Bodø's main mall. Space for pre-dinner drinks or an after-work cocktail. Lunchtime buffet on Friday. Good sushi and pizzas.

Børsen Spiseri $$ *Svinøya Rorbuer, Gunnar Bergs vei 2, Svolvær, Lofoten Islands, tel: 76-06 99 30,* www.svinoya.no. Housed in the main reception building of Svinøya's traditional fishing cabin company, Børsen offers traditional Lofoten cuisine, in a rustic romantic setting, overlooking the fjord. The Taste of Lofoten plate serves as a good introduction to the islands' cuisine, including Lofoten lamb, stockfish, whale and even some local cheeses.

Bryggeri Kaia $$ *Sjøgaten 1, Bodø, tel: 75-52 58 08.* Bodø's best eatery, set right on the harbour – grilled-meat buffet, speciality tapas and seafood platters to choose from. Outdoor seating by the waterfront and a piano bar functions at the weekends.

Dromedar Kaffebar $$ *Nordregate 2, Trondheim, tel: 73-53 00 60.* A lovely place to drop in for breakfast, lunch or an excellent cup of coffee with cake. The brownies and scones are particularly good.

Hagen $ *Nedre Bakklandet 75, Trondheim, tel: 405-44 309.* Popular, affordable lunchtime buffet with a wide choice of delicious vegan and vegetarian dishes, including salads, sandwiches and burgers, that appeal to non-vegetarians too.

Havfruen $$ *Kjøpmannsgata 7, Trondheim, tel: 73-87 40 70,* www.havfruen. no. Trondheim's premier fish and seafood restaurant, housed in one of the old buildings along Nidelva River. Excellent food in a lovely setting.

Johnsens Ferksvare $$ *Storgata 78, Leknes, tel: 76-08 18 55.* A superb, down-to-earth fish restaurant serving all kinds of fresh seafood, and some great starters such as olive bread and smoked salmon.

Vertshuset Røros $$–$$$ *Kjerkgata 34, Røros, tel: 72-41 93 50*, www. vertshusetroros.no. Situated in a traditional inn, this restaurant emphasises organic food and fresh, local produce. Sample menus include a Taste of Central Norway. The inn serves breakfast, lunch and dinner daily, and also has accommodation (16 double rooms and seven apartments).

THE FAR NORTH

Arctic Restaurant & Bar $$ *Scandic Kirkenes Hotel, Kongensgate 1-3, Kirkenes, tel: 78-99 59 00*, www.scandichotels.no. Arctic and international cuisine inside the modern Scandic Kirkenes Hotel in the town centre. À la carte menu; open for breakfast, lunch and dinner.

Emmas Drømmekjøkken $$–$$$ *Kirkegata 8, Tromsø, tel: 77-63 77 30*, www.emmas.as. The name literally means 'Emma's Dream Kitchen'. Innovative cooking, beautifully presented, with new takes on Norwegian classics, run by an excellent team of female chefs.

Kongsfjord Gjestehus $$ *Veines, Kongsfjord, tel: 78-98 10 00*, www. kongsfjord-gjestehus.no. Home-cooked, traditional Norwegian dishes with an emphasis on fish and seafood dishes. Marinated whale steak is sometimes on the menu. Local cloudberries and home-made cheesecake are on the dessert menu.

Thai House Restaurant $$ *Storgata 22, Tromsø, tel: 77-67 05 26*, www. thaihouse.no. Unusual though it sounds, this is authentic Thai cooking in the Arctic. Open for lunch and dinner. Eat in or takeaway food. Also has a sister restaurant of the same name in Tromsø.

A-Z TRAVEL TIPS

A SUMMARY OF PRACTICAL INFORMATION

A

ACCOMMODATION (see also Camping, Youth Hostels and the list of Recommended Hotels starting on page 134)

The standard of hotels is generally good in Norway with a range of comfortable accommodation available. Prices can be quite steep, since many hotels are geared towards the business traveller. There are considerable discounts in summer or at weekends, when hotels do special offers to attract business customers. In recent years smaller, family-run hotels have been bought up by international chains. This does not appear to have worsened the standard, and if anything it has made prices somewhat more competitive. Bear in mind the main tourist season in Norway is quite short and not all accommodation options are available year-round, although this is changing.

As well as hotels there are a number of other accommodation options, in rural areas in particular, such as guesthouses and B&Bs, farm- and home-stays, youth hostels, campsites and, perhaps the most popular of all, a cottage, cabin or holiday home, the so-called *hytte*. Networks such as the Historic Hotels and Restaurants, *De Historiske* (www.dehistoriske.com), have a number of unusual character hotels across the country. In some parts along the coast, for example the Lofoten Islands, it is possible to stay in old fishing cabins, *rorbuer*, or even in a lighthouse. Norway's most extensive hotel pass is the Fjord Pass, offering discounts at almost 100 places nationwide, www.fjordtours.com. The Norwegian Tourist Board has good advice on places to stay and there is an online booking service at www.visitnorway.com.

I'd like a single/double room. **Jeg vil gjerne ha et enkelt/ dobbeltrom**

with bath/shower **med bad/dusj**

How much is the room? **Hvor mye koster rommet?**

AIRPORTS

Norway's main airports are Oslo Gardermoen, Bergen Flesland, Stavanger Sola and Trondheim Værnes. Oslo is also served by Torp near
Sandefjord. Because of the distances and topography, domestic flights
are a good option for getting around and the country is well served by
domestic carriers. There are 16 primary airports, several of which are
served by international flights, and 29 regional airports. Taxis from the
main airports tend to be quite expensive.

Oslo Gardermoen is 50km (31 miles) north of the city centre and has
only one terminal serving both domestic and international flights (tel:
67-03 00 00, www.avinor.no). There are plenty of eateries, duty-free
shops, exchange facilities, tourist information and a car hire desk.
The quickest way to the centre of Oslo is the Gardermoen Line Airport
Express Train, *Flytoget*, taking 19 minutes and running six times an
hour to the Central Station. There are also regular commuter trains
operated by Norwegian State Railway, airport coaches and a taxi
rank outside the airport. Ryanair and other low-cost carriers fly into
Torp airport (www.torp.no), near Sandefjord, 110km (68 miles) south
of Oslo. Coaches are laid on to coincide with the flights and take approximately 2–2.5 hours. There are also trains to Sandefjord with a bus
shuttle to the airport.

Bergen Flesland is 20km (12 miles) south of Bergen. It has all the usual
facilities. A frequent airport bus runs from the bus station and the central Radisson hotels to the airport, taking approximately half an hour
(www.bergen-guide.com).

Stavanger Sola lies 15km (9 miles) southwest of the centre and has a
conference centre plus the usual facilities. The airport bus takes 20–30
minutes and there are taxis (tel: 67-03 00 00, www.avinor.no).

Trondheim Værnes, 35km (22 miles) north of Trondheim centre, has
shops and restaurants, a hotel, meeting and conference facilities, as
well as exchange facilities. The airport can be reached by train, airport
express bus, regular bus service or taxi. Travel time is around 35–40
minutes (tel: 67-03 00 00, www.avinor.no).

> Where can I get a taxi? **Hvor kan jeg finne en taxi?**
> How much is it to downtown Oslo? **Hvor mye koster det til Oslo sentrum?**
> Does this bus/train go to Oslo? **Går denne bussen/dette toget til Oslo?**

B

BICYCLE HIRE

Bikes are easy to rent, from specialist rental shops or local tourist offices, guesthouses and hotels. Roads tend to be fairly empty and the bigger cities have cycle paths. Bear in mind that the mountain terrain can be challenging. Towns and villages are sometimes few and far between, particularly in the far north, and the weather is very changeable. Rental prices vary widely, depending on the quality of the bike and the area – anything from NOK100–250 a day. Tourist offices usually have good maps and information on bike routes. Two scenic routes are the North Sea Cycle Route and the Navvies' Road. Bike Norway has further information, www.cyclingnorway.no.

BUDGETING FOR YOUR TRIP

Prices differ between the cities and rural areas, as well as from high season to low season, and prices given here are only approximate. As a rule the cities tend to be more expensive than the countryside, with a few exceptions such as around the best-known fjords.

Car hire. Prices vary considerably. Rates for seven days' hire vary from around NOK3,000 for a small car to NOK4,000 for a large car. Most companies provide child seats, for an additional charge.

Hotels. Average rates per night can be divided into budget, medium and up-market (based on two people sharing and including breakfast): NOK1,100, NOK1,100–1,800 and over NOK1,800. Prices can be well below the NOK1,100 bracket, but also rise well above NOK1,800. There are plenty of special offers, weekend rates and packages for visitors.

Meals and drinks. Breakfast in a café or restaurant costs NOK50–100; lunch NOK60–150; dinner at a medium-priced restaurant, not including drinks, NOK200–250 per head; coffee or soft drink NOK20–30; bottle of wine from NOK150; spirits (4cl) NOK80. Hotel breakfasts and lunches are both good bets, as the former is substantial and restaurants often do a dish of the day at lunchtime.

Museums. NOK60–150. Children usually get 50 percent discount.

Petrol. NOK15.70 per litre and diesel NOK14.70. Most petrol stations have automatic pumps that take notes and credit/debit cards.

Public transport. Transport is comparatively expensive in Norway, but both buses and trains are of a high standard of comfort. The average price for a train ticket Oslo–Bergen is NOK600.

Taxis. Taxis are expensive. Average cost from Gardermoen Airport to Oslo city centre is NOK610–720, depending on the time of day.

Tourist cards. The Oslo Pass and the Bergen Card are cards giving free entry to a variety of sights, plus access to free public transport and many other benefits. For further information see www.visitoslo.com and www.visitbergen.com. Visit Norway has information on all passes and tourist cards, www.visitnorway.com.

C

CAMPING

Norway has some 1,000 campsites, graded from one to five stars. Most campsites are open June–August only, with a few open longer, including year-round for caravans and mobile homes. Many sites also have cabins for hire on a weekly basis in summer. Costs for camping range from NOK 100–200 per day with an additional fee for electricity hook-up. The Norwegian Camping Card and the Scandinavian Camping Card can be bought at all participating sites and offer discounts, swift registration at sites and other advantages. A Camping Card International is accepted as an equivalent. The website of www.camping.no has useful information. Norway's Right of Public Access law means you may put up a tent or sleep under stars anywhere in the countryside in open, unfenced land, for a maximum of 48 hours, as long as you are at least 150 metres/yds from the nearest house or cabin. If you want to stay longer you need the owner's permission. Also bear in mind that open fires are not allowed near forested areas 15 April–15 September.

CAR HIRE

All the major car hire companies are represented in Norway, including Avis, Europcar and Hertz, and there are also local Norwegian car hire firms with competitive rates. Most towns of any size have car hire companies, or cars can easily be hired directly at airports, either booked in advance or upon arrival. Rates are generally cheaper the longer you hire the car for, and there are often special rates in summer or at weekends. It's usually possible to pick up a hire car in one place and drop it off in another. To hire a car you will need a full valid licence from your country of residence, held for at least a year. If a non-EU citizen, you may need an International Driver's Permit (IDP). You must be at least 19 years of age to hire a car, but if you are under 25 years of age you may need to pay a young driver's fee of approximately NOK 100 per day. Insurance is mandatory so check that this is included in the cost of the car hire.

I'd like to rent a car. **Jeg vil gjerne leie en bil.**
tomorrow **i morgen**
for one day/week **for en dag/uke**
Please include full insurance. **Vær så snill og inkludere komplett forsikring**.

CLIMATE

The Gulf Stream gives Norway a milder climate than the latitude might indicate, with temperatures sometimes reaching 25–30°C (77–86°F) in summer. Temperatures vary widely between winter and summer, north and south, coast and interior, sea level and mountain peaks. The weather is very changeable too, and in many parts of the country they joke about having 'all seasons in one day'. Late June to mid-August, the weather tends to be sunny with temperatures in the mid-20s°C (mid-70s°F) and sea temperatures reaching 15–18°C (59–65°F), except in the far north. This is the time to see the midnight sun in the Arctic regions. Spring and autumn are slightly cooler and wetter. Autumn is when you can start to observe the Northern Lights, *aurora borealis*, best in October, February and March. In winter a lot of Norway, except the coast, is snow-covered and inland temperatures can drop as low as -40°C (-40°F). It may rain any time of year on the coast, and even in summer temperatures can drop to 10°C (50°F), particularly in the evening.

Average daytime temperatures in Celsius:

	Oslo	Bergen	Trondheim	Bodø	Tromsø
Jan	-2.3	2.7	-1.6	-1.3	-3.8
Feb	-1.3	3	-0.7	-0.9	-3.1
Mar	2.4	4.9	2.1	-1	-1
Apr	7.3	8	5.1	3.8	1.7
May	14	12.9	10.5	8.5	6.1
June	17.6	15.1	13.2	11.8	11
July	19.9	16.6	15.3	14.1	13.7
Aug	18.7	16.3	14.9	13.8	12.5
Sept	13.7	13.3	11.3	10.7	8.4
Oct	8.1	9.8	6.7	6	3.3
Nov	2.3	5.8	1.8	1.7	-1
Dec	-1.4	3.3	-1.1	-0.5	-3

CLOTHING

It's a good idea to wear several layers and be prepared for differences in temperature. Even on a sunny day it's worth having an umbrella and waterproofs, along with sunglasses and sunhat. Norwegians are generally informal, so shorts and a T-shirt are fine for sightseeing on a warm day. Take extra layers for the evening or if taking a boat trip. Good footwear is essential not only for hiking trails and outdoor activities, but for cobblestones in many cities. During winter, thermals, boots, a coat, scarves, gloves and hats are essential.

CRIME AND SAFETY

Norway is a comparatively safe country, with low crime rates, particularly in terms of violent crime, and it's rare that visitors experience any form of crime. In rural areas crime tends to be burglaries or petty theft. Take the same precautions you would at home, look after your belongings, especially in crowded areas and on public transport, and don't walk alone at night in unlit areas of bigger cities.

D

DRIVING

The roads are usually well maintained and quiet, with the exception of the bigger cities, but even there traffic jams are rare. Winter tyres are obligatory in winter (dates vary depending on location). Some roads in the far north are closed in winter. In spring, when the ground frost thaws, some roads can be challenging to drive along. There are also a number of long tunnels, including the world's longest at 24.5km (15 miles), in the mountainous areas.

Speed limits. The general speed limit is 80kph (50mph). In residential areas it is 30kph (18mph); in built-up areas 50kph (30mph); on dual carriageways and motorways 90 or 100kph (55 or 62mph). Caravans and trailers may not exceed 80kmh (50mph) even if the local speed limit is higher.

Documents. A full valid licence from your home country, held for at least a year, is required, or an International Driver's Permit if your licence was issued outside the EU/ECA.

Rules. Drive on the right, pass on the left, and give way to traffic from the right, unless otherwise indicated. Seat belts are obligatory, both in front and back seats. Headlights must be dipped at all times. Drink-driving laws are strict and spot checks are common. The alcohol limit is 0.2 milligrams per litre of blood, so it's best to avoid alcohol altogether or you run the risk of being over the limit, which attracts high fines and the risk of losing your licence.

Accidents and breakdowns. You must carry a red warning triangle and yellow fluorescent vest in case of breakdown or accident. For emergency repairs and technical assistance: Norges Automobil-Forbund (NAF), tel: 23-21 31 00, Falken, tel: 02222 (freephone), or Viking, tel: 06000 (freephone).

Are we on the right road for...? **Er dette veien til...?**
My car has broken down. **Bilen min har fått motorstopp.**
There's been an accident. **Det har vært en ulykke.**
Driving/driver's licence **førerkort**
Stop **stopp**
Crossroads **veikryss**
Dangerous curve/bend **farlig kurve**
Parking allowed/No Parking **parkering tillatt/forbutt**
Drive carefully **Kjør forsiktig**
Bus stop **bussholdeplass**
Danger **Fare**
No entry **Ingen inngang**
No through road/one-way street **enveisgate**
Roadworks **veiarbeid**

E

ELECTRICITY

220 volts AC, standard two-pin, round continental plugs. Visitors should bring their own adaptors.

EMBASSIES, CONSULATES AND HIGH COMMISSIONS

Australia: Most services are dealt with by the Australian Embassy in Denmark, tel: (+45) 70-26 36 76, www.denmark.embassy.gov.au.

Canada: Wergelandsveien 7, N-0244 Oslo, tel: 22-99 53 00, www.canada international.gc.ca/norway-norvege.

Ireland: Haakon VIIs gate 1, N-0244 Oslo, tel: 22-01 72 00, www.dfa.ie/irish-embassy/norway.

New Zealand: the New Zealand Embassy in the Netherlands handles enquiries from Norway, tel: (+31) 70-346 9324, www.nzembassy.com.

South Africa: Drammensveien 88 C, N-0271 Oslo, tel: 23-27 32 20, www.saemboslo.no.

UK: Thomas Heftyes gate 8, N-0244 Oslo, tel: 23-13 27 00, www.gov.uk/world/organisations/british-embassy-oslo.

US: Morgedalsvegen 36, N-0378 Oslo, tel: 21-30 85 40, https://no.us embassy.gov.

Most embassies and consulates are open Mon–Fri 8.30am–4.30pm.

Where can I find the British/American/Canadian/Australian/South African embassy? **Hvor kan jeg finne den britiske/amerikanske/kanadensiske/australiensiske/sørafrikanske ambassaden?**

EMERGENCIES

The police can be reached by dialling 112, ambulance and urgent medical assistance on 113 and the fire brigade on 110. For non-urgent police matters dial 02800.

G

GETTING TO NORWAY

Air. Many international carriers have flights to Norway, either direct or via a hub, including SAS, British Airways, Norwegian, KLM, Lufthansa and Thai Airways. Domestic flights are operated by SAS, Norwegian and Widerøe.

Sea. There are ferries between Norway and Denmark, operated by Color Line (www.colorline.com), DFDS Seaways (www.dfdsseaways.co.uk), Fjordline (www.fjordline.com) and Stena Line (www.stenaline.co.uk), as well as Oslo to Kiel in Germany and from Strömstad in Sweden to Sandefjord, both operated by Color Line. In Norway there are numerous ferries and boats along the coast: the best known is Hurtigruten, running from Bergen to Kirkenes in the far north (www.hurtigruten.co.uk or www.hurtigruten.com).

Rail. One option for travelling to, from and around Norway is to get a rail pass, such as an Interrail (for Europeans) or Eurail (for non-Europeans) Global Pass. These must be booked before leaving your country and are offered by InterRail, www.interrail.eu, or Eurail, www.eurail.com (for general European rail tickets).

GUIDES AND TOURS

English is widely spoken in Norway, so it is easy to find English-speaking guides and tours. Many bus or boat tours and museums have multilingual guiding in Norwegian, English, German, French

We need an English-speaking guide **Vi trenger en engelsktalende guide.**

and increasingly in Russian, Mandarin and Japanese. Tourist offices can book tours and guides, and provide multilingual leaflets about the tours available. Some of the most popular tours, such as Norway in a Nutshell, are organised by Nutshell Tours and Fjord Tours (www.norwaynutshell.com and www.fjordtours.com). Visit Norway has a useful list of tourist offices at www.visitnorway.com.

H

HEALTH AND MEDICAL CARE

Norway is a member of the EEA (the European Economic Area), which entitles all visitors from other member countries to the same medical care as Norwegian citizens. EU/EEA nationals should bring a European Health Insurance Card (EHIC) available in the UK through post offices or online at www.ehic.org.uk; it is free and valid for five years. Travel insurance is highly recommended for all visitors. Make sure this covers you for winter or adventure sports, if you plan to engage in these. There are no vaccinations required for Norway and tap water is safe to drink.

There is a 24-hour pharmacy *(apotek)* in Oslo: Jernbanetorvet Pharmacy, Jernbanetorget 4B, Oslo, tel: 23-35 81 00.

Where can I find the nearest (all-night) pharmacy? **Hvor kan jeg finne det nærmeste (24-timers) apotek?**
I need a doctor/dentist/an ambulance **Jeg trenger en doktor/tannlege/ambulanse**
hospital **hospital/sykehus**
I have an upset stomach **Jeg har mavepine**
a fever **feber**
headache **hodepine**
cold/flu **førkjølelse/influensa**

HOLIDAYS

New Year's Day 1 January
Maundy Thursday March/April
Good Friday March/April
Easter Monday March/April
Labour Day 1 May
Constitution/National Day 17 May
Ascension Day May/June
Whit Monday late May/early June
Christmas Day 25 December
Boxing Day 26 December

L

LANGUAGE

Norwegian has two official written forms, *bokmål* (literally 'book language') and *nynorsk* ('new Norwegian'). Some 86 percent primarily use *bokmål*. Across Norway more than 20,000 people also speak various Sami languages, part of the Finno-Ugric language group and not related to Norwegian. English is widely spoken and taught in schools from a young age.

Hello **Hei**
Good Morning **God Morgen**
Good Day **Goddag**
Good Evening **God Kveld**
Goodbye **Ha det**
Yes **Ja**
No **Nei**
How are you? **Hvordan går det?**
I'm fine **Det går bra**
Nice to meet you **Hyggelig å treffe deg**

Thank you **Takk**
You're welcome **Ingen årsak**
Excuse me **Unnskyld**
Sorry **Beklager**
Please **Vær så snill**
My name is... **Jeg heter...**
Do you speak English? **Snakker du engelsk?**
I don't speak Norwegian **Jeg snakker ikke norsk**
Cheers! **Skål!**
January **januar**
February **februar**
March **mars**
April **april**
May **mai**
June **juni**
July **juli**
August **august**
September **september**
October **oktober**
November **november**
December **desember**
Monday **Mandag**
Tuesday **Tirsdag**
Wednesday **Onsdag**
Thursday **Torsdag**
Friday **Fredag**
Saturday **Lørdag**
Sunday **Søndag**

Learning a few useful phrases of Norwegian, although not essential, is very much appreciated. Pronunciation can be a challenge and Norwegian has an additional three vowels, at the end of the alphabet – æ, ø and å. Å is pronounced like the English 'o' in 'cold', æ like 'ai' in 'hair', ø like 'ea' in 'heard'.

LGBTQ TRAVELLERS

Both the legal framework and the general attitude towards lesbian, gay, bisexual and transgendered people are fairly liberal in Norway. Most LGBTQ travellers do not experience any problems or hassle, but bear in mind that Norway is not a very populous country and there isn't much of an LGBTQ scene or community outside the main cities, and even there, bars and clubs can be a bit thin on the ground. The liberal attitude doesn't always extend to the smaller, more rural communities, although it's rare that anyone experiences any overt discrimination. FRI – the Norwegian Organization for Sexual and Gender Diversity, Tollbugata 24, tel: 23 10 39 39, https://foreningenfri.no (in Norwegian only) has more information. Visit Oslo also has an LGBTQ section on their website, www.visitoslo.com/en/your-oslo/gay-oslo.

M

MAPS

Most local tourist offices have got good maps of their particular area. Another option is Stanfords in the United Kingdom, tel: (+44) 207-836 1321, www.stanfords.co.uk.

MEDIA

Radio and television. There are two main television companies, the state-run NRK with four channels, and TV2, also with four channels. All programmes are shown in original language with subtitles. National radio is also dominated by NRK, which has three radio channels broadcasting over FM and DAB.

Newspapers and magazines. According to Reporters Without Borders, Norway ranks number one in worldwide press freedom. The main dailies are *Aftenposten*, *Dagbladet* and *Dagsavisen*, and there is a large number of local newspapers and magazines. *The Norway Post* (www. norwaypost.no) publishes news from Norway in English.

MONEY

Currency. Norwegian currency is the *krone* (plural *kroner*), made up of 100 *øre*. It is abbreviated kr or NOK (the international abbreviation). Coins come in 50 *øre*, 1, 5, 10 and 20 *kroner*. Banknotes come in 50, 100, 200, 500 and 1,000 *kroner*.

Exchange facilities. You can exchange money at airports and at Oslo's Central Station, as well as many commercial and savings banks, some post offices, branches of Forex and some hotels. Forex is the main bureau de change (usually open Mon–Fri 8am–8pm, Sat 9am–5pm).

Credit and debit cards. Most major credit and debit cards are accepted even in smaller establishments. This makes it easier to avoid carrying large quantities of cash. ATMs are easy to find and easy to use and all towns of any size have at least one, but in remote areas it's best to have some cash with you.

Reporting lost or stolen credit cards:

American Express, tel: 0800-68 100

Diners Club, tel: 021-01 50 00

Mastercard, tel: 0800-30 250

VISA, tel: 0815-00 500

Traveller's cheques. Traveller's cheques are gradually becoming less common, but can still be exchanged at banks, Forex and other bureaux de change. Banks usually give better rates.

> Can I pay by credit card? **Kan jeg få betale med kredittkort?**
> I want to change some money/pounds/dollars/euros into Norwegian kroner **Jeg vil gjerne veksle penger/pund/ dollar/euros til norske kroner.**

Where's the nearest bank/bureau de change? **Hvor ligger nærmeste bank/vekselkontor?**
Is there a cash machine/ATM near here? **Finnes det en bankomat i nærheten?**
How much does it cost? **Hvor mye koster det?**

Tipping. It is usual to round up a restaurant or bar bill to the nearest 5 or 10 *kroner*, but it's rarely frowned upon if you don't. Ten percent in bars and restaurants is reasonable if you have received good service. Taxi drivers sometimes receive slightly higher tips, whereas tipping is not expected at the hairdressers, for example.

O

OPENING TIMES
Shops. Most shops are open Mon–Fri 10am–5pm or 6pm, Sat 9am–2pm. Shops in bigger cities and large malls or department stores stay open later, until 8pm or 9pm, and also open on Sunday. Some shops still close for lunch, particularly in rural areas, and it's common for smaller, privately owned shops to close for summer holidays for two weeks or more in July or August.

Banks. Banks are open Mon–Fri 9am–3.30pm, and Thu until 5pm. In the summer months (mid-May–mid-Aug), banks close at 2.30pm all week, but bureaux de change stay open later.

P

POLICE
Most police stations are open weekdays and have a desk where the public can report crime or other incidents. The emergency number for the police is 112 and this is free when calling from a payphone.

> Where's the nearest police station? **Hvor er den nærmeste politistasjon?**
> I've lost my wallet/bag/passport/documents. **Jeg har mistet lommeboken min/posen min/passet mitt/ dokumenterne mine.**

POST OFFICES

Norwegian postboxes are red for both national and international mail. Most post offices are open Mon–Fri 8am–5pm and Sat 9am–3pm, closed on Sunday.

> Where's the nearest post office? **Hvor er nærmeste postkontor?**

PUBLIC TRANSPORT

Norway has good public transport connections to most parts of the country, but in some rural areas and the far north, a car or boat can be a necessity for getting from A to B.

By Air. Due to the long distances, flying is one of the best options for getting around Norway. There are some 50 airports, serving even very small communities. The main carriers for domestic flights are SAS (www.flysas.com), Norwegian (www.norwegian.com) and Widerøe (www.wideroe.no).

By Train. Norwegian State Railways, NSB, covers 3,000km (1,864 miles), as far north as Bodø. Several journeys are particularly scenic such as the Bergen Line, from Oslo to Bergen, the Rauma railway from Dombås to Åndalsnes, and the Flåm Railway from Myrdal to Flåm. For information and tickets see www.nsb.no.

By Bus. A number of bus companies operate in Norway, the largest of which is Nor-Way Bussekspress with 40 routes (www.nor-way.no). Tickets can be bought online or at bus stations. You are allowed to take bikes and skis on board buses for a fee, provided there is space. Many buses are scheduled so that they connect with onward-going ferries or intersecting bus routes.

By Ferry/Boat. A myriad ferry and boat companies operate along the coastline. Many of these are express boats or car ferries connecting the fjordlands and the many islands with the mainland. It's often necessary to hop on a ferry across a fjord since this is quicker than driving to the nearest bridge, and many roads have ferry connections. Hurtigruten, Fjord1, Fjordline, Kolumbus and Rødne Fjordcruise are some of the main operators.

By Car. See Driving, page 119.

Where can I get a taxi? **Hvor kan jeg finne en taxi?**
Where is the nearest bus stop? **Hvor er nærmeste bussholdeplass?**
When's the next bus to...? **Når går neste buss til...?**
I would like a ticket to... **Jeg vil gjerne ha en billet til...**
single/return **enkel/tur-retur**

R

RELIGION

Around 80 percent of the population are Protestants, belonging to the state Lutheran Church. This figure is somewhat misleading as one becomes a member when baptised and in reality Norway is one of the most secular nations in Europe with people attending church only once or twice a year. Some 10 percent of the population do not belong to any organised form of religion and the remainder belong to a variety of faiths from the Sami shamanistic religion to Bahá'i.

T

TELEPHONE

Public phones taking coins, phonecards or credit cards, and are easy to find in main cities and towns. Phonecards are sold in newsagents, 7Elevens and similar stores. Off the beaten track, including the far north, payphones are harder to find. Taking your own mobile, or, for longer stays, buying a Norwegian SIM card, are good options, but beware of steep roaming rates and lack of reception. For citizens of 31 European Economic Area countries, including the UK and Ireland, roaming charges for temporary roaming were abolished in mid-2017 yet under a fair use policy some restrictions on the free use of mobile phones are still in place.

TIME ZONE

Norway keeps Central European Time, one hour ahead of Greenwich Mean Time, with Daylight Saving Time from late March to late October, when clocks go forward by one hour.

New York	London	Paris	**Oslo**	Sydney	Auckland
6am	11am	noon	**noon**	8pm	10pm

TOILETS

There are plenty of clean, well-kept public toilets in cities; most are coin operated and charge around NOK5. In rural areas toilets are harder to find, but service stations, areas near main squares or tourist offices are usually a good bet and mostly free. Along highways there are lay-bys or rest areas with toilet facilities, but off the beaten track and along smaller roads, toilets are nonexistent.

Excuse me, where is the toilet? **Unnskyld, hvor er toalettet?**

TOURIST INFORMATION

Innovation Norway, the Norwegian Tourist Board, www.visitnorway.com, has 16 main tourist information offices in Norway and there is a large number of local tourist information offices across the country, although some are only open in summer. All display the international tourist sign (white 'i' on green background). Staff are knowledgeable, often multilingual, and can provide information about the area and make bookings for accommodation and tours. There are usually also leaflets and maps available in various languages.

In Norway:

Central Station Tourist Information, Jernbanetorget 1, Oslo (July–Aug Mon–Sat 8am–7pm, Sun 9am–6pm, rest of the year shorter hours), tel: 81-53 05 55, www.visitoslo.com.

Bergen, Strandkaien 3, Bergen, tel: 55-55 20 00, www.visitbergen.com.

Stavanger, Strandkaien 61, Stavanger, tel: 51-85 92 00, www.regionstavanger-ryfylke.com.

Tromsø, Kirkegata 2, Tromsø, tel: 77-61 00 00, www.visittromso.no.

Trondheim, Nordregata 11, Trondheim, tel: 73-80 76 60, www.visittrondheim.no.

For information on the **Western Fjords**, visit www.fjordnorway.com.

Overseas:

Innovation Norway has offices in 30 countries worldwide.

In the UK: Innovation Norway, West End House, 11 Hills Place, London W1F 7SE, tel: (+44) 207-839 8800, www.visitnorway.com.

In the US: Innovation Norway, 655 Third Avenue, New York, NY 10017, tel: (+1) 212-885 9700, www.visitnorway.com.

V

VISAS AND PASSPORTS

EU citizens only need a valid passport to visit Norway, which is a member of the Schengen agreement. Visitors from Canada, Australia, USA and New Zealand do not need a tourist visa for stays of under 90 days.

Other nationalities should check with their Norwegian embassy. A visitor's visa is usually valid for three months.

W

WEBSITES AND INTERNET CAFÉS

Most tourist information websites have information in English (and additional languages). The following is a list of useful websites:

www.visitnorway.com

www.visitoslo.com

www.visitbergen.com

www.fjordnorway.com

www.regionstavanger-ryfylke.com

www.trondheim.com

www.trondelag.com

www.nordnorge.com

www.lofoten.info

www.cyclingnorway.no

www.norwegian.com

www.visitflam.com

www.hurtigruten.co.uk and www.hurtigruten.com

There is internet access at most airports and stations. Hotels, restaurants, cafés and bars increasingly have Wi-fi.

Y

YOUTH HOSTELS

Norway has more than 100 hostels, run by two different chains – Hostelling International (www.hihostels.no) and VIP Backpackers Resorts International (www.vipbackpackers.com). Dormitories range from NOK100–00, a double room from NOK300–800. Hostels usually provide duvets and pillows, but bring your own linen or sleeping bag. Most hostels provide very good value for money.

RECOMMENDED HOTELS

Norway has a variety of accommodation from luxury establishments to youth hostels, and typically standards are high, often with prices to match. International chains have taken over a number of hotels, but as a rule the character has remained unchanged. Choice hotels (www.nordicchoicehotels.no) and Best Western (www.bestwestern.no) tend to be of better quality in Norway than in many other places and have some of the best city locations. In the fjordlands and the countryside there are still many smaller guesthouses and B&B accommodation. Sometimes family-run, they are often more reasonably priced and in scenic settings. Some of the best hotels are members of the Historic Hotels and Restaurants network – manor houses, boutique hotels and old coaching inns, for example (www.dehistoriske.com). Renting a cottage *(hytte)* is also an option, and can reduce accommodation and food costs substantially (www.norsc.co.uk). For those on an even stricter budget, hiring a camper van/mobile home or simply taking a tent is another option. Campsites are plentiful, although the season is short, especially in the far north. In the bigger cities hotels are open year-round, but some smaller guesthouses open only during the summer season.

The price categories are based on two people sharing a double room at full rates including breakfast, MOMS (VAT) and service charge.

$$$	over NOK1,800
$$	NOK1,100–1,800
$	below NOK 1,100

OSLO

Best Western Karl Johan $$ *Karl Johansgate 33, tel: 23-16 17 00,* www. bestwestern.com. One of the most centrally located hotels in Oslo, opposite parliament, with excellent views.

Citybox Oslo $ *Prinsens gate 6, tel: 21-42 04 80*, www.citybox.no. Budget traveller's hotel located just next to the central railway station and just a few minutes' walk from Aker Brygge, known for its cafés and nightlife. All rooms equipped with shower and Wi-fi.

Clarion Collection Hotel Folketeateret $$ *Storgaten 21–3, tel: 22-00 57 00*, www.nordicchoicehotels.no. Central hotel with 160 rooms in an attractive Art Deco building. A light evening buffet is included in the room price.

Cochs Pensjonat $ *Parkveien 25 Oslo, tel: 23-33 24 00*, www.cochspensjonat.no. Good-value family-run guesthouse close to the Royal Palace. Three different types of rooms, some with a kitchenette and fridge for self-catering.

First Hotel Grims Grenka $$$ *Kongens Gate 5 Oslo, tel: 23-10 72 00*, www.firsthotels.com. This design hotel has 65 rooms including suites, a rooftop lounge for cocktails and a restaurant that serves Scandinavian specialities.

First Hotel Millennium $$$ *Tollbugata 25, tel: 21-02 28 00*, www.firsthotels.com. Well-appointed hotel a short walk from Karl Johan. There are 114 rooms and excellent conference and meeting facilities.

Hotell Bondeheimen $$$ *Rosenkrantz Gate 8, tel: 23-21 41 00*, www.bondeheimen.com. Central hotel with 127 pleasant rooms in an historic building. The 100-year-old café, Kaffi-stova, serves traditional Norwegian cuisine and there is a good handicraft shop attached.

THE SOUTH AND SOUTHEASTERN BORDERLANDS

Gaustablikk Hotell $–$$ *Rjukan, tel: 35-09 14 22*, www.gaustablikk.no. Mountain lodge at the foot of southern Norway's highest peak. It is a ski centre in winter. Also has cabins sleeping up to 16 people.

Grand Hotell Halden $–$$ *Jernbanetorget 1, Halden, tel: 69-18 72 00*. The oldest hotel in Halden, dating from the 1850s, the Grand has 33 rooms. At the time of writing these were being extensively refurbished and upgraded.

Hotel Norge $$ *Dronningens Gate 5, Kristiansand, tel: 38-17 40 00*. Centrally located hotel with good spa facilities. Also does cooking courses in the Gladkjøkkenet restaurant.

STAVANGER AND AROUND

Clarion Collection Hotel Amanda $$ *Smedasundet 93, Haugesund, tel: 52-80 82 00*, www.nordicchoicehotels.no. Intimate hotel offering organic breakfasts and a light evening buffet. Sauna and health club facilities.

Darby's Inn $$ *Oscarsgate 18, Stavanger, tel: 47-62 42 58*, www.darbysbb. com. This clean and cosy, centrally located bed and breakfast is run by charming hosts and has beautifully-furnished rooms.

Energihotellet $–$$ *Nesflaten, tel: 51-20 05 55*, www.energihotellet.no. Design hotel located in a former hydrostation. Twenty-nine rooms, 14 of which overlook Suldalsvatnet Lake.

Skagen Brygge Hotell $$$ *Skagenkaien 28–30, Stavanger, tel: 51-85 00 00*, www.nordicchoicehotels.no. In the heart of the harbour, one of the best locations in Stavanger. Good atmosphere and excellent cocktail bar facing the quayside.

Stavanger Bed & Breakfast $ *Vikedalsgaten 1A, Stavanger, tel: 45 41-31-60*, www.stavangerbedandbreakfast.no. Budget accommodation a short walk from the cathedral; 22 rooms. Free Wi-fi, bumper breakfasts and coffee with waffles in the evenings.

BERGEN AND AROUND

Augustin Hotel $–$$ *C. Sundts Gate 22, Bergen, tel: 55-30 40 00*, www. augustin.no. Centrally located with 113 rooms; free Wi-fi and free waffles. Cosy basement wine bar and restaurant.

Grand Hotel Terminus $$ *Zander Kaaesgate 6, Bergen, tel: 55-21 25 00,* www.grandterminus.no. Elegant hotel near the station. It has reputedly the best whisky bar in Norway; there are stone-baked pizzas as well as gourmet dining.

Hanseatic Hotel Bergen (Det Hanseatiske Hotel) $–$$ *Finnegården 2A, Rosenkrantzgaten 6, Bergen, tel: 55-30 48 00,* www.dethanseatiskehotell. no. Within the Bryggen Unesco World Heritage Site; 37 individual rooms with classic wooden interiors.

Solstrand Fjord Hotel $$$ *Osøyro, Os, tel: 56-57 11 00,* www.solstrand. com. Beautiful historic hotel and spa on the Bjørnefjord, 30km (19 miles) south of Bergen. Outdoor and indoor pools and a variety of treatments available.

Thon Hotel Sandven $$ *Norheimsund, tel: 56-55 20 88,* www.thonhotels. no. Worth a visit for its 150-year history alone. It has 102 individually designed rooms and a floating café on Hardangerfjord.

CENTRAL NORWAY AND THE WESTERN FJORDS

Brakanes Hotel $$ *Ulvik, Hardanger, tel: 56-52 61 05,* www.brakanes -hotel.com. A grand old dame of a hotel with 142 comfortable rooms, many with balconies overlooking the fjord.

Dr Holms Hotel $$$ *Timrehaugveien 2, Geilo, tel: 32-09 57 00,* www. drholms.no. Member of the Historic Hotels network, it has a long and distinguished history. Some of the 125 rooms are decorated in English romantic style and the spa is renowned.

Fossheim Hotell $–$$ *Lom, tel: 61-21 95 00.* Traditional hotel in an old-fashioned wooden building. Gourmet dining and good walking in nearby Jotunheimen national park. Closed mid-December to mid-February.

Hotel Brosundet $$ *Apotekergata 5, Ålesund, tel: 70-10 33 00,* www.bro sundet.no. Room options include the Molja lighthouse on the harbour. The restaurant serves excellent seafood.

Quality Hotel $$ *Gravensteinsgata 5, Sogndal, tel: 57-62 77 00*, www.nordicchoicehotels.no. Large, well-equipped hotel a short walk from Sogndal bus station. Three restaurants with a wide choice of dishes, from pizzas to Norwegian specialities.

Tørvis Hotel $$ *Marifjøra, tel: 57-68 72 00*. Old-fashioned, white-painted building in a manor-house style, complete with well-kept gardens for alfresco meals. Situated right on the Lustrafjord near a small beach and pier.

Vangsgaarden Guesthouse $ *Aurland, tel: 57-63 35 80*, www.vangsgaarden.no. A cluster of quaint buildings in the village of Aurland, it includes a guesthouse, a motel, pub and several fjord cabins *(rorbuer)*, beautifully situated on the Aurlandsfjord.

Walaker Hotel $$ *Solvorn, tel: 57-68 20 80*, www.walaker.com. Norway's oldest family-run hotel has been in the hands of the same family since 1690. It is part of the Historic Hotels network and has rooms in the main building, in the annex and in a small cottage nearby. Well known for its romantic garden and home-cooked local specialities.

TRØNDELAG AND NORDLAND

Å Rorbuer & Brygga Restaurant $–$$ *Å i Lofoten, Sørvågen, Lofoten Islands, tel: 76-09 11 21*. These picturesque fishing cabins, painted a bright red, are situated in one of Lofoten's most authentic old fishing villages, with 33 listed buildings and several of the islands' best museums.

Britannia Hotel $$ *Dronnigens Gate 5, Trondheim, tel: 73-80 08 00*, www.britannia.no. The oldest hotel in Trondheim, built in 1897, gets its name from the era when British aristocracy came here for a spot of salmon fishing. The hotel will reopen in 2019 after a major restoration.

Clarion Collection Hotel Grand Olav $$ *Kjøpmannsgate 48, Trondheim, tel: 73-80 80 80*, www.nordicchoicehotels.no. This centrally located hotel, a short walk from the main square and the Nidelva River, is known as

Backstage Hotel since most rooms are individually decorated by different artists. Free Wi-fi, DVDs in the rooms, and organic breakfasts.

Quality Hotel Grand Royal $$ *Kongensgate 64, Narvik, tel: 76-97 70 00,* www.nordicchoicehotels.no. This central Narvik hotel has 162 high-quality rooms and two restaurants and can organise killer-whale safaris and fishing trips. In winter it is only a short distance from good skiing, including off-piste.

Røros Hotell $$ *An-Magrittsvei, Røros, tel: 72-40 80 00,* www.roroshotell. no. The largest hotel in the region with 157 rooms. Close to the centre and good hiking trails. Facilities include a dance floor, playroom for children, pool and sauna.

Scandic Nidelven $$ *Havnegata 1, Trondheim, tel: 73-56 80 00,* www. scandichotels.com. Large, modern hotel, on River Nidelva, near Trondheim's newest shopping area; 343 well-equipped rooms, and the hotel officially has Norway's best breakfast buffet.

Singsaker Sommerhotell $ *Rogerts Gate 1, Trondheim, tel: 73-89 31 00,* https://sommerhotell.singsaker.no. Open only in summer (mid-June to mid-Aug), student accommodation during the rest of the year, Singsaker has 103 rooms sleeping 1–4 people, or dormitory style. Breakfast is included.

Skagen Hotel $$ *Nyholmsgata 11, Bodø, tel: 75-51 91 00,* www.skagen-hotel.no. Comfortable hotel located in two adjacent buildings, connected by an underground tunnel. Close to the town centre; free Wi-fi.

Stamsund Rorbuer $ *Stamsund, Lofoten Islands, tel: 952-38 072,* www. stamsundrorbuer.no. A collection of 19 former fishing cabins (*rorbuer*), some more than 100 years old, each sleeping 4–8 people. Beautiful location on Vestfjorden.

Svinøya Rorbuer $–$$ *Gunnar Bergs vei 2, Svolvær, Lofoten Islands, tel: 76-06 99 30,* www.svinoya.no. Svinøya has 30 different fishing cabins, from standard to de luxe, situated on a small island near the centre of Svolvær. There is also an excellent restaurant attached to the main building.

THE FAR NORTH

Arctic Cabins $ *Vestvatn, Misvær, tel: 901-71 002,* www.arctic-cabins.no. Scenic cabins and accommodation in a tranquil setting of Saltfjellet/ Svartise national park. A stay can be combined with fishing tours or dog sledding (see page 84).

Batsfjord Brygge $$ *Strandveien, Båtsfjord, tel: 78-98 32 83.* Five nice, simply-furnished cabins, with kitchenettes, each sleeping 4–8 people. Perfect for getting away from it all, with hiking trails on the doorstep.

Kongsfjord Gjestehus $ *Veines, Kongsfjord, tel: 78-98 10 00,* www.kongs fjord-gjestehus.no. A converted farmhouse and fishermen's quarters dating back to the end of the 18th century, this guesthouse has a quiet, cosy atmosphere and is open year-round. There is a nearby gallery, and boat trips and diving excursions can also be arranged.

Scandic Ishavshotel $$ *Fr Langesgate 2, Tromsø, tel: 77-66 64 00,* www. scandichotels.no. Set right on the harbour, Ishavshotel offers great views of the fjord and the Arctic Cathedral opposite. It has 214 modern, well-appointed rooms, scrumptious breakfasts, and lies within easy walking distance of the main sights.

SVALBARD

Radisson Blu Polar Hotel Spitsbergen $$$ *Road 500, Longyearbyen, Svalbard, tel: 79-02 34 50,* www.radissonblu.com. The world's northern-most full-service hotel with 95 rooms and apartment suites. There are unparalleled glacier views, and the hotel can help book and organise Svalbard packages, including outdoor activities and air transport.

DICTIONARY

ENGLISH–NORWEGIAN

adj adjective   **adv** adverb   **BE** British English   **n** noun   **prep** preposition   **v** verb

A

a (common nouns) en; **(neuter nouns)** et
access (internet) v bruke (internett)
accessories tilbehør
accident ulykke
accommodation innkvartering
account konto
acetaminophen paracetamol
acupuncture akupunktur
adapter adapter
address adresse
admission adgang
after etter
afternoon ettermiddag
air conditioning klimaanlegg
airline flyselskap
airmail luftpost
airport flyplass
aisle midtgang
aisle seat sete ved midtgangen
all alt
allergic allergisk
allergic reaction allergisk reaksjon
allowed tillatt
alter v endre
alternate route annen rute
aluminum foil aluminiumsfolie
amazing praktfull
ambulance sykebil

American adj amerikansk; n amerikaner
amusement park fornøyelsespark
anemic blodfattig
antibiotic antibiotikum
antique antikvitet
antiques store antikvitetshandel
antiseptic cream antiseptisk salve
any noe
anyone noen
anything noe
apartment leilighet
appetizer forrett
appointment avtale
arcade spillehall
area område
area code retningsnummer
aromatherapy aromaterapi
around (nearby) rundt
arrival ankomst
arrive v komme fram
arthritis leddgikt
ask v spørre
aspirin aspirin
asthma astma
at ved
ATM minibank
attack overfall
attractive tiltrekkende
automatic adj automatisk

B

baby baby
baby bottle tåteflaske

baby wipes papirkluter
babysitter barnevakt
back adv (direction) tilbake; n (body part) rygg
backpack ryggsekk
bag (carrier) bærepose
baggage [BE] bagasje
baggage claim bagasjemottak
bakery bakeri
bandage bandasje
bank (finance) bank
bar (place) bar
barber herrefrisør
basket (store) handlekurv
basketball basketball
bathroom bad
battery batteri
battleground slagsted
be v være
beach strand
beautiful vakker
bed seng
before før
beginner begynner
behind bak
beige beige
belt belte
best best
bicycle sykkel
big stor
bike route sykkelsti
bikini bikini
bill regning
birthday fødselsdag
black svart
bland smakløs

blanket ullteppe
bleed v blø
blind blind
blood blod
blood pressure blodtrykk
blouse bluse
blue blå
boat båt
boarding ombordstigning
boarding pass ombordstigningskort
book bok
bookstore bokhandel
boring kjedelig
botanical gardens botanisk hage
bother v plage
bottle flaske
bottle opener flaskeåpner
bowl (container) bolle
boy gutt
boyfriend kjæreste
bra behå
bracelet armbånd
break down v (car) få motorstopp
breakfast frokost
breathe v puste
bridge bro
briefs underbukse
bring v (something) ta med
British britisk
broken (bone) brukket; **(out of order)** gått i stykker

brooch brosje
broom feiekost
brown brun
bug (insect) insekt
bus buss
bus station busstasjon
bus stop bussholdeplass
business forretning
business card visittkort
business center forretningssenter
busy opptatt
but men
buy v kjøpe; (treat) by på

C

cable car n taubane
cafe kafé
call n (phone) samtale;
   v (phone) ringe
camera kamera
camp v campe
campsite n campingplass
can v (be able to) kunne;
   n (container) boks
can opener boksåpner
cancel v annullere
candlestick lysestake
car bil
car hire [BE] bilutleie
car park [BE] parkeringsplass
car rental bilutleie
car seat barnesete
carafe karaffel
card kort
cardigan (Norwegian) lusekofte
carry v bære
carry-on (luggage) håndbagasje
cart (shopping) handlevogn; (luggage) tralle
carton kartong
cash v løse inn; n kontanter

cashier kasse
castle slott
cathedral domkirke
cave hule
cell phone mobil
certificate of authenticity ekthetssertifikat
chair stol
chair lift stolheis
change v (alter) endre; (baby) bytte på; (transport) bytte; v (money) veksle; n (money) vekselpenger
cheap billig
check (payment) sjekk; (restaurant) regning
check in v (airport) sjekke inn
check-in desk innsjekkingskranke
check out v sjekke ut
cheers skål
cheese slicer ostehøvel
chemical toilet kjemisk toalett
chemist [BE] apotek
cheque [BE] sjekk
chest bryst
chest pain vondt i brystet
chewing gum tyggegummi
child barn
children's menu barnemeny
children's portion barneporsjon
church kirke
cigar sigar
cigarette sigarett
cinema [BE] kino
city by
classical music klassisk musikk
clean adj ren; v vaske
cleaning supplies rengjøringsmidler

clear v (ATM) slette
cliff klippe
cling film [BE] plastfolie
close v stenge
closed stengt
clothing store klesbutikk
coat (man's) frakk;
   (woman's) kåpe
coin mynt
cold adj kald; n (illness) forkjølelse
colleague kollega
color farge
comb kam
come v komme
computer datamaskin
concert konsert
conditioner (hair) hårbalsam
condom kondom
conference konferanse
confirm v bekrefte
constipation forstoppelse
contact lens kontaktlinse
contact lens solution kontaktlinsevæske
convention hall konferansesenter
contain v inneholde
control n kontroll
cooking facilities kokemuligheter
copper kobber
corkscrew korketrekker
corner hjørne
cost v koste
cot [BE] (child's) sprinkelseng
cotton bomull
cough hoste
country land
country code landkode
countryside land
cover charge inngangspenger
cream (ointment) salve

credit card kredittkort
crib (child's) barneseng
crystal krystall
cup kopp
currency valuta
currency exchange office vekslingskontor
customs toll
cut v (with scissors) klippe
cute søt
cycling sykling
cycling race sykkelløp

D

dairy melkeprodukter
damage v skade
dance v danse
dance club diskotek
dark mørk
day dag
deaf døv
deck chair fluktstol
declare v (customs) fortolle
deep dyp
delay forsinkelse
delayed forsinket
delete v (computer) slette
delicatessen delikatesseforretning
denim dongeri
dentist tannlege
denture gebiss
deodorant deodorant
department store stormagasin
departure avgang
deposit (down payment) depositum
detergent vaskemiddel
diabetic diabetiker
diamond diamant
diaper bleie
diarrhea diarré

dictionary ordbok
diesel diesel
difficult vanskelig
digital digital
digital camera digital-kamera
digital photo digitalt bilde
digital print papirkopi av et digitalt bilde
dinner middag
direction retning
dirty skitten
disabled bevegelses-shemmet
discount rabatt
dish n (plate) fat; (food) rett
dish detergent oppvaskmiddel
dishwasher oppvask-maskin
display case monter
disposable camera engangskamera
disposable razor engangshøvel
dive v dykke
diving equipment dykkeutstyr
divorced skilt
dizzy svimmel
do v gjøre
doctor lege
dog hund
doll dukke
dollar dollar
domestic innenlands
door dør
double dobbel
double bed dobbeltseng
double room dobbeltrom
down ned
downtown sentrum
drag lift skitrekk
dress kjole
dress code kleskode

drink v drikke; n drikk
drink menu drikkekart
drive v kjøre
driver's license førerkort
driving licence [BE] førerkort
drop (liquid) dråpe
drowsiness søvnighet
dry tørr
dry cleaner renseri
dummy [BE] (baby's) narresmokk
duty (customs) toll
duty-free tollfri

E

earache øreverk
earring ørering
east øst
easy lett
eat v spise
economy class turistklasse
electrical outlet strømuttak
elevator heis
e-mail n (message) e-post; v sende e-post
e-mail address e-postadresse
emergency exit nødutgang
empty adj tom; v tømme
end n slutt; v slutte
English engelsk
English-speaking engelsktalende
engrave v gravere
enjoy v nyte
enter v gå inn
equipment utstyr
escalator rulletrapp
e-ticket e-billett
excess luggage overvek-tig bagasje
evening kveld
event begivenhet

exchange v veksle
exchange rate vek-slingskurs
excursion utflukt
excuse v unnskylde
exit n utgang
expensive dyr
express ekspress
express mail ekspresspost
extension (phone) linje
extra ekstra
extra large ekstra stor
eye øye
eyebrow øyenbryn

F

face ansikt
facial ansiktsbehandling
family familie
fan (appliance) vifte
far langt
farm bondegård
fast hurtig
fax n faks; v fakse
fax number faksnummer
fee gebyr
feed v mate
ferry ferge
ferry landing fergested
fever feber
field jorde
fill (a prescription) v gjøre i stand
fill out v fylle ut
fill up v fylle
filling (tooth) plombe
fine (OK) fin
fire (open) ild; (disaster) brann
fire door branndør
first class første klasse
fit v passe
fitting room prøverom
fix v reparere
fjord fjord
flight flyavgang

floor etasje
flower blomst
folk music folkemusikk
food mat
foot fot
football [BE] fotball
football game [BE] fotballkamp
for for
forest skog
fork gaffel
form (document) skjema
formula morsmelker-statning
fountain fontene
free fri
freezer fryser
fresh fersk
friend venn
from fra
frying pan stekepanne
full full
full time heltid

G

game (match) kamp
garbage bag søppelsekk
garden hage
gas (car) bensin
gas station bensinstasjon
gate utgang
get v (find) få tak i
get off v gå av
get to v komme til
gift gave
gift shop gavebutikk
girl jente
girlfriend kjæreste
give v gi
glacier bre
glass (drinking) glass
glasses (optical) briller
go v gå
go away v gå vekk
go out v gå ut
gold gull

golf golf
golf club golfkølle
golf course golfbane
golf tournament golfturnering
good god
good afternoon god dag
good evening god aften
good morning god morgen
good night god natt
goodbye adjø
gram gram
grandchild barnebarn
gray grå
green grønn
greeting hilsen
grocery store dagligvarebutikk
ground floor første etasje
guesthouse pensjonat
guide guide
guide dog førerhund
gym trimrom

H

hair hår
hair salon frisørsalong
hairbrush hårbørste
haircut klipp
hairdresser frisør
hairspray hårlakk
halal halal
half halv
handbag håndveske
handicapped handikappet
hard hard
hat hatt
have v ha
head hode
headache hodepine
health food store helsekostbutikk
health insurance sykeforsikring
hearing impaired hørselshemmet

heart hjerte
heart condition hjertesykdom
heat varme
heater varmeovn
heavy tung
heel hæl
hello hallo
helmet hjelm
help n hjelp; v (assist) hjelpe; (oneself) ta selv
here her
high høy
highchair babystol
highway motorvei
hill høyde
hire n utleie; v leie
hold on v (phone) vente litt
holiday helligdag; [BE] ferie
horse hest
hospital sykehus
hot varm
hotel hotell
hour time
house hus
how hvordan
how far hvor langt
how long hvor lenge
how late hvor sent
how many hvor mange
how much hvor mye
hungry sulten
hurry n hastverk
hurt v gjøre vondt
husband ektemann

I

I jeg
ibuprofen ibuprofen
icy kaldt
identification legitimasjon
ill [BE] syk
important viktig
impressive imponerende

in i
include v inkludere
indoor pool innendørs svømmebasseng
inexpensive rimelig
information informasjon
information desk informasjonsskranke
insect insekt
insect bite insektstikk
insect repellent insektmiddel
insert v sette inn
inside inni
instant messenger lynmelder
insurance forsikring
insurance claim forsikringskrav
interesting interessant
international internasjonal
internet internett
internet cafe internettkafé
interpreter tolk
intersection veikryss
introduce v (person) presentere
iron (clothing) strykejern

J

jacket jakke
jazz jazz
jeans olabukse
jet-ski vannscooter
jeweler gullsmed
jewelry smykker
join v (go with somebody) bli med
just (only) bare

K

keep v beholde
key nøkkel
key card nøkkelkort
kiddie pool plaskebasseng
kilo kilo

kilometer kilometer
kiss v kysse
knife kniv
know v (something) vite; (somebody) kjenne
kosher koscher
krone (Norwegian currency) krone

L

lace knipling
lactose intolerant laktoseintolerant
lake innsjø
language språk
large stor
last sist
late sen
later senere
launderette [BE] selvbetjeningsvaskeri
laundromat selvbetjeningsvaskeri
laundry (place) vaskeri; (clothes) vask
laundry facilities vaskemuligheter
lawyer advokat
leather lær
leave v (depart) dra; (deposit) legge igjen
leave alone v la være i fred
left (direction) venstre; (remaining) igjen
lens (for glasses) glass
less mindre
lesson lærdom
letter brev
library bibliotek
life boat livbåt
life jacket flytevest
lifeguard badevakt
lift [BE] (elevator) heis
lift pass heiskort

light *adj* **(weight)** lett;
adj **(color)** lys; *n* lys
light bulb lyspære
lighter lighter
like *v* like
line linje
linen **(cloth)** lin
liquor store vinmonopol
liter liter
little **(some)** litt
live *v* **(exist)** leve;
(reside) bo
live music levende musikk
loafers mokkasiner
local lokal
lock lås
log in *v* logge seg inn
log off *v* logge seg av
log on *v* logge seg på
long lang
look *n* titt; *v* se
lose *v* miste
loud **(voice)** høy
love *v* elske
low lav
luggage bagasje
luggage cart bagasjetralle
luggage locker op-
pbevaringsboks
luggage trolley **[BE]**
bagasjetralle
lunch lunsj

M

machine maskin
machine washable
maskinvaskbar
magazine blad
magnificent storslagen
mail post
mailbox postkasse
make *v* lage
make up **(a prescription)**
[BE] *v* gjøre i stand
mall kjøpesenter
man mann; **(gentleman)**

herre
manager **(shop)** butikksjef
manicure manikyr
many mange
map kart
market marked
married gift
mass **(church)** messe
match **(matchstick)**
fyrstikk; **(sport)** kamp
massage massasje
may **(can)** kunne
meal måltid
mean *v* bety
measuring cup målebeger
measuring spoon
måleskje
medication legemiddel
medium mellomstor
meet *v* møtes
meeting møte
meeting room møterom
memory card minnebrikke
mend *v* lappe
menstrual cramps
menstruasjonssmerter
menu meny
message beskjed
meter meter
microwave mikrobølgeovn
midday **[BE]** middag
midnight midnatt
mileage kjørelengde
minute minutt
miss *v* mangle
missing savnet
mistake feil
mobile **(phone)** mobil
moment øyeblikk
money penger
month måned
mop mopp
moped moped
more mer
morning morgen
mosque moské

motion sickness reisesyke
motorcycle motorsykkel
motorboat motorbåt
motorway **[BE]** motorvei
mountain fjell
mouth munn
move *v* flytte
movie film
movie theater kino
much mye
mug *v* overfalle
mugging overfall
museum museum
music musikk
must **(have to)** måtte

N

nail **(human)** negl
nail file neglefil
nail salon neglesalong
name navn
napkin serviett
nature preserve
nasjonalpark
nauseous uvel
near nær
nearby i nærheten
necklace halskjede
need *v* trenge
new ny
newspaper avis
next neste
next to ved siden av
night natt
nightclub nattklubb
no nei; **(not anything)**
ikke noe
no one ingen
non-alcoholic alkoholfri
non-carbonated kullsyrefri
non-smoking **(area)** for
ikke-røykere
noon middag
north nord
Norway Norge
Norwegian *n* nordmann;

adj norsk
not ikke
nothing ingenting
notify *v* underrette
novice nybegynner
now nå
number **(shoes)** nummer;
(counting) tall
nurse sykepleier

O

off av
off-licence **[BE]**
vinmonopol
office kontor
office hours kontortid
old gammel
on på
once én gang
one en
one-way ticket
enveisbillett
only bare
open *v* åpne; *adj* åpen
opera opera
opposite midt imot
optician optiker
order *v* **(meal)** bestille
other andre
outdoor pool utendørs
svømmebasseng
outlet **(electric)** stikkontakt
overlook utsikt
overnight natten over

P

p.m. **(afternoon)** om ettermiddagen; **(evening)**
om kvelden
pacifier **(baby's)** narresmokk
pack *v* pakke
package pakke
paddling pool **[BE]**
plaskebasseng

pain smerte
pajamas pyjamas
palace slott
pants langbukse
panty hose strømpebukse
paper papir
paper towel husholdningspapir
paracetamol [BE] paracetamol
park n park; v parkere
parking lot parkeringsplass
part time deltid
pass through v være på gjennomreise
passport pass
passport control passkontroll
password passord
pastry bakverk
pastry shop konditori
path sti
pay v betale
peak topp
pearl perle
pediatrician barnelege
pedicure fotpleie
pen penn
penicillin penicillin
pensioner pensjonist
per day per dag
per hour per time
per kilometer per kilometer
per night per natt
per week per uke
perfume parfyme
period (menstruation) menstruasjon
permit v tillate
petrol [BE] bensin
petrol station [BE] bensinstasjon
pewter tinn
pharmacy apotek

phone telefon
phone call telefonsamtale
phone card telefonkort
phone number telefonnummer
photo foto
photocopy fotokopi
photograph fotografi
pick up v (person) hente
picnic picnic
picnic area turområde
piece stykke
pill pille; (contraceptive) p-pille
pillow pute
pink rosa
piste [BE] løype
piste map [BE] løypekart
place n (location) sted; (in hostel) plass
plastic wrap plastfolie
plate tallerken; (dessert) asjett
platform [BE] (station) perrong
play n (theatre) stykke; v spille
playground lekeplass
playing card spillkort
playpen lekegrind
please adv vær så snill
plunger klosettpumpe
pocket lomme
point v peke
point of interest severdighet
poles (ski) staver
police politi
police report politirapport
police station politistasjon
pond dam
pop music popmusikk
portion porsjon
possible mulig

post (mail) [BE] post
postage stamp frimerke
postbox [BE] postkasse
postcard postkort
post office postkontor
pot gryte
pound (British currency) pund
pregnant gravid
premium (gas) super
prepaid calling time ringetid
prescription resept
press v (iron) presse
pressure trykk
price pris
print v skrive ut; n (photo) kopi
problem problem
pronounce v uttale
pronunciation uttale
pull v trekke
purple fiolett
push v (open) skyve
pushchair [BE] gåstol
put v sette
put through sette over

Q

question spørsmål
quick rask
quickly øyeblikkelig
quiet rolig

R

racecourse [BE] travbane
racetrack travbane
racket (sport) racket
railway station [BE] jernbanestasjon
rain n regn; v regne
raincoat regnfrakk
rainy regnfull
rap (music) rap
rape voldtekt
rash utslett

rate (exchange) kurs
razor barberhøvel
razor blade barberblad
reach v nå
ready klar
real (genuine) ekte
receipt kvittering
receive v motta
recommend v anbefale
red rød
refrigerator kjøleskap
region område
regular (fuel) normalbensin
reindeer skin reinsdyrskinn
relationship forhold
rent v leie
rental car leiebil
repair v reparere
repeat gjenta
report n rapport; v (a crime) anmelde
reservation bestilling
reserve v bestille
restaurant restaurant
restroom toalett
retired (from work) pensjonert
return v (come back) komme tilbake; (give back) levere tilbake
return ticket [BE] turreturbillett
right (correct) rett; (direction) høyre
ring (jewelry) ring
river elv
road vei
road map veikart
road sign trafikkskilt
rob rane
romantic romantisk
room rom
room service romservice
round (golf) runde

round-trip ticket tur-returbillett
route rute
rowboat robåt
rubbish [BE] søppel
rubbish bag [BE] søppelsekk
ruin ruin

S

safe *adj* (free from danger) trygg; *n* safe
sandals sandaler
sanitary napkin sanitetsbind
saucer skål
sauna badstue
save (computer) lagre
scarf skjerf
schedule (transport) rutetabell
scissors saks
sea sjø
sealskin slippers selskinntøfler
seat plass
see *v* (watch) se; (meet) treffe; (examine) undersøke
sell *v* selge
seminar seminar
send *v* sende
senior citizen pensjonist
separately hver for seg
separated separert
sentence setning
serve *v* servere
service service; (church) gudstjeneste
shampoo sjampo
should burde
sheet laken
ship *n* skip; *v* sende
shirt skjorte
shoe store skobutikk
shoes sko

shop butikk
shopping area handlestrøk
shopping centre [BE] butikksenter
shopping mall butiksenter
shopping trolley [BE] handlevogn
short kort
shorts shorts
show *v* vise
shower dusj
shrine helligdom
sick (ill) syk
side side
side effect bivirkning
sightseeing sightseeing
sightseeing tour sightseeingtur
sign *v* undertegne
silk silke
silver sølv
single (unmarried) ugift
single room enkeltrom
single ticket [BE] enveisbillett
size (clothes) størrelse; (shoes) nummer
ski *v* gå på ski
skis ski
ski lift skiheis
skirt skjørt
slice skive
slippers tøfler
slow langsom
slowly langsomt
small liten
smoke røyke
smoking (area) for røykere
sneakers turnsko
snorkeling equipment snorkleutstyr
snow *n* snø; *v* snø
snowboard snøbrett
snowshoes truger
soap såpe

soccer fotball
soccer game fotballkamp
sock sokk
someone noen
something noe
somewhere et eller annet sted
soon snart
sore throat sår hals
sorry *v* beklage
south sør
souvenir suvenir
souvenir store suvenirbutikk
spa spa
speak *v* snakke
speciality spesialitet
spoon skje
sports idrett
sports massage idretts-massasje
sprained forstuet
square plass
stadium stadion
stairs trapp
stamp *v* stemple; *n* (postage) frimerke
start *v* starte
station stasjon
stay *v* (remain) bli; (reside) bo
steal *v* stjele
steep bratt
sterling silver sterlingsølv
stocking strømpe
stolen stjålet
stomach mage
stomachache magesmerte
stop *n* (place) holdeplass; *v* stoppe
store (shop) butikk
store directory butikkguide
stove komfyr
straight ahead rett frem
strange underlig
stream bekk

street gate
stroller gåstol
student student
study *v* studere
stunning overveldende
style *v* (hair) style
subway T-bane
subway station T-banestasjon
suit *n* (man's) dress; (woman's) drakt
suitable passende
suitcase koffert
sun sol
sunburn solforbrenning
sunglasses solbriller
sunscreen solkrem
sunstroke solstikk
super (gas) superbensin
supermarket supermarked
surfboard surfebrett
swallow *v* svelge
sweater genser
swelling hevelse
swim *v* svømme
swimming pool svøm-mebasseng
swimming trunks badebukse
swimsuit badedrakt
symbol tegn
synagogue synagoge

T

table bord
tablet (medical) tablett
take *v* ta
tampon tampong
taste *v* smake
tax skatt
taxi drosje
taxi rank [BE] drosje-holdeplass
taxi stand drosjeholdeplass
team lag
teaspoon teskje

tell v si
temple (religious) tempel
tennis tennis
tennis court tennisbane
tennis match tenniskamp
tent telt
terminal (airport) terminal
terrible forferdelig
text n tekst; v (message) tekste
than enn
thank v takke
theft tyveri
there (place) der; (direction) dit
these disse
thief tyv
thing ting
think v (believe) tro
this denne; dette
those de
throat hals
ticket billett
ticket office billettluke
tights [BE] strømpebukse
time (period) tid; (occasion) gang
timetable [BE] rutetabell
tissue papirlommetørkle
to (direction) til; (time) på
tobacco tobakk
tobacconist tobakkshandel
today i dag
toilet [BE] toalett
toilet paper toalettpapir
tomorrow i morgen
tonight i kveld
too for
tooth tann
toothache tannpine
toothbrush tannbørste
toothpaste tannpasta
tour tur
tourist office turistkontor

towel håndkle
town by
town map bykart
town square torg
toy leketøy
toy store leketøysbutikk
track (railway) spor
traditional tradisjonell
traffic light trafikklys
trail løype
trail map løypekart
train tog
train schedule togtabell
train station jernbanestasjon
tram trikk
translate v oversette
trash søppel
travel v reise
travel agency reisebyrå
travel guide reisehåndbok
travel sickness reisesyke
traveler's check reisesjekk
trim (hair) stuss
trip tur
troll troll
trousers [BE] langbukse
try on v prøve
T-shirt T-skjorte
turn off (device) skru av
turn on (device) skru på
TV TV
type v (computer) skrive
typically typisk

U

ugly stygg
umbrella paraply
underground [BE] n T-bane
underground station [BE] T-banestasjon
undershirt trøye
understand v forstå
unleaded blyfri
until til

upset stomach urolig mage
use n bruk; v bruke
username brukernavn

V

vacation ferie
vacuum cleaner støvsuger
vaginal infection underlivsbetennelse
valley dal
value verdi
VAT [BE] moms
vegetarian vegetarianer
very meget
viking ship vikingskip
visit n besøk; v (a person) besøke
visiting hours besøkstid
visually impaired synshemmet
volleyball game volleyballkamp
vomit v kaste opp

W

wait v vente
waiter servitør
waitress servitør
wake v vekke
wake-up call vekking
walk v (go) gå; (stroll) spasere
wallet lommebok
want v ville
warm adj varm; v varme
wash v vaske
washable vaskbar
washing mashine vaskemaskin
watch klokke
water vann
waterfall foss
water skis vannski
weather vær
weather forecast værutsikter

week uke
weekend helg
welcome velkommen
west vest
what hva
wheelchair rullestol
wheelchair ramp rullestolsrampe
when når
where hvor
which hvilken
white hvit
who hvem
whole hel
widowed (man) enkemann; (woman) enke
wife kone
window vindu
window seat vindusplass
windsurfer seilbrett
wine list vinkart
wireless internet trådløst internett
with med
withdraw v (from account) ta ut
without uten
woman kvinne
wooden figurine trefigur
wool ull
work v (toil) arbeide; (function) virke
wrap up v pakke inn
write v skrive
wrong i veien

Y

year år
yellow gul
yes ja
yesterday i går
you du
youth hostel vandrerhjem

Z

zoo dyrehage

NORWEGIAN-ENGLISH DICTIONARY

A

adapter adapter
adjø goodbye
adresse address
advokat lawyer
akkurat nå right now
akupunktur acupuncture
alkoholfri non-alcoholic
allergisk allergic
allergisk reaksjon
 allergic reaction
alt all
aluminiumsfolie
 aluminum foil
amerikaner n American
amerikansk adj American
anbefale v recommend
andre other
ankomst arrival
anmelde v report (a theft)
annen rute alternate route
annullere v cancel
ansikt face
ansiktsbehandling facial
antibiotikum antibiotic
antikvitet antique
antikvitetshandel
 antiques store
antiseptisk salve
 antiseptic cream
aperitiff aperitif
apotek pharmacy
 [chemist BE]
arbeide v work
armbånd bracelet
aromaterapi aromatherapy
asjett plate (dessert)
aspirin aspirin
astma asthma
automatisk automatic
av off
avgang departure

avis newspaper
avtale appointment

B

baby baby
babystol highchair
bad bathroom
badebukse swimming
 trunks
badedrakt swimsuit
badevakt lifeguard
badstue sauna
bagasje luggage [baggage BE]
bagasjemottak baggage
 claim
bagasjetralle luggage
 cart [trolley BE]
bak behind
bakeri bakery
bakverk pastry
bandasje bandage
bank bank (finance)
bar n bar (place)
bare just; only
barn child
barnebarn grandchild
barnelege pediatrician
barnemeny children's
 menu
barneporsjon children's
 portion
barnesete car seat
barnevakt babysitter
basketball basketball
batteri battery
be om v ask for
begivenhet event
begynner beginner
beholde v keep
behå bra

beige beige
bekk stream
beklage v be sorry
bekrefte v confirm
belte belt
bensin gas (petrol
 BE) (car)
bensinstasjon gas
 [petrol BE] station
beskjed message
best best
bestille v order (meal);
 reserve
bestilling reservation
besøk n visit
besøke v visit (someone)
besøkstid visiting hours
betale v pay
bety v mean
bevegelseshemmet
 disabled
bibliotek library
bikini bikini
bil n car
billett ticket
billettluke ticket office
billig cheap
bilutleie car rental
 (hire BE)
bivirkning side effect
blad magazine
bleie diaper
bli v stay (remain)
bli med v join (someone)
blind blind
blod blood
blodfattig anemic
 (anaemic BE)
blodtrykk blood pressure
blomst flower
bluse blouse
blyfri unleaded
blø v bleed

blå blue
bo live (reside); stay
 (reside)
bok book
bokhandel bookstore
boks can (container)
boksåpner can opener
bolle bowl
bomull cotton
bondegård farm
bord table
botanisk hage botanical
 gardens
bra fine (OK)
brann fire (disaster)
branndør fire door
bratt steep
bre glacier
brev letter
briller glasses
britisk British
bro bridge
brosje brooch
bruk n use
bruke v use
brukernavn username
brukket broken (bone)
brun brown
bryst chest
burde should
buss bus
bussholdeplass bus stop
busstasjon bus station
butikk store [shop BE]
butikkguide store directory
butikksenter shopping
 mall [centre BE]
butikksjef manager (shop)
by n city; town
bykart town map
bytte v change (transportation)
bytte på v change (baby)

bære v carry
bærepose bag (carrier)
båt boat

C

campe v camp
camping camping
campingplass campsite

D

dag day
dagligvarebutikk grocery store
dal valley
dam pond
danse v dance
dansk Danish
datamaskin computer
delikatesseforretning delicatessen
deltid part time
denne this
deodorant deodorant
depositum deposit (down payment)
der there (place)
dette this
diabetiker diabetic
diamant diamond
diarré diarrhea
die breastfeed
diesel diesel
digital digital
digitalkamera digital camera
digitalt bilde digital photo
diskotek dance club
disse these
dit there (direction)
dobbel double
dobbeltrom double room
dobbeltseng double bed
dollar dollar
domkirke cathedral
dongeri denim
dra v leave (depart)

drakt suit (woman's)
dress suit (man's)
drikk n drink
drikke v drink
drikkekart drink menu
drosje taxi
drosjeholdeplass taxi stand [rank BE]
dråpe drop (liquid)
du you
dukke doll
dusj shower
dykke v dive
dykkeutstyr diving equipment
dyp adj deep
dyr adj expensive
dyrehage zoo
dør door
døv deaf

E

e-billett e-ticket
ekspert expert
ekspress express
ekspresspost express mail
ekstra extra
ekstra stor extra large
ekte real (genuine)
ektemann husband
ekthetssertifikat certificate of authenticity
elske v love
elv river
en a (common nouns); one
engangshøvel disposable razor
engangskamera disposable camera
engelsk English
engelsktalende English-speaking
enke widowed (woman)
enkeltrom single room
enkemann widowed (man)

enn than
enveisbillett one-way [single BE] ticket
e-post e-mail
e-postadresse e-mail addess
erfaren experienced
et a (neuter nouns)
et eller annet sted somewhere
et øyeblikk hold on (phone)
etasje floor
etter after
ettermiddag afternoon

F

faks n fax
fakse v fax
faksnummer fax number
familie family
farge color
fat dish
feber fever
feiekost broom
feil mistake
ferge ferry
ferie vacation [holiday BE]
fersk fresh
film movie
fiolett purple
fjell mountain
fjord fjord
flaske bottle
flaskeåpner bottle opener
fluktstol deck chair
fly flight
flyplass airport
flyselskap airline
flytevest life jacket
flytte v move
folkemusikk folk music
fontene fountain
for for; too
for røykere smoking (area)
forferdelig terrible
forhold relationship

forkjølelse cold (illness)
fornøyelsespark amusement park
forretning business
forretningssenter business center
forrett appetizer
forsikring insurance
forsikringskrav insurance claim
forsinkelse delay
forsinket delayed
forstoppelse constipation
forstuet sprained
forstå v understand
fortolle v declare (customs)
foss waterfall
fot foot
fotball soccer [football BE]
fotballkamp soccer [football BE] game
foto photo
fotokopi photocopy
fotpleie pedicure
fra from
frakk coat (man's)
fri free
frimerke stamp (postage)
frisør hairdresser
frisørsalong hair salon
frokost breakfast
fryser freezer
full full
fylle v fill up
fylle ut v fill out
fyrstikk match (matchstick)
fødselsdag birthday
før before
førerhund guide dog
førerkort driver's license [driving licence BE]
første etasje ground floor
første klasse first class

få motorstopp v break down (car)

få tak i v get (find)

G

gaffel fork

gammel old

gang n time (occasion)

gate street

gave gift

gavebutikk gift shop

gebiss denture

gebyr fee

genser sweater

gi v give

gift adj married

gir n speed (cycle)

gjenta v repeat

gjøre v do

gjøre i stand v make up (prepare)

gjøre vondt v hurt

glass glass (drinking)

glass lens (for glasses)

god god

god aften good evening

god dag good afternoon

god morgen good morning

god natt good night

godter candy

golf golf

golfbane golf course

golfkølle golf club

golfturnering golf tournament

gram gram

gravere v engrave

gravid pregnant

gryte pot

grå gray

grønn green

gudstjeneste service (church)

guide guide

gul adj yellow

gull n gold

gullsmed jeweler

gult gull yellow gold

gutt boy

gå v go; walk

gå av v get off

gå inn v enter

gå på ski v ski

gå seg bort v get lost

gå ut v go out

gå vekk go away

gåstol stroller [pushchair, buggy BE]

gått i stykker broken (out of order)

H

ha v have

ha det travelt v be in a hurry

ha gått seg bort v be lost

hage garden

halal halal

hallo hello

hals throat

halskjede necklace

halv half

halvtime half an hour

handikappet handi-capped

handlekurv basket (shopping)

handlestrøk shopping area

handlevogn shopping cart [trolley BE]

hans his

hard hard

haste v to be urgent

hatt hat

heis elevator [lift BE]

heiskort lift pass

hel n whole

helg weekend

helligdag holiday

helligdom shrine

helsekostbutikk health food store

heltid full time

hennes her

hente v pick up (person)

her here

herre man (gentleman)

herrefrisør barber

hest horse

hevelse swelling

hilsen greeting

hjelm helmet

hjelp n help

hjelpe v help

hjerte heart

hjertesykdom heart condition

hjørne corner

hode head

hodepine headache

holde rundt hug

holdeplass stop (place)

hoste v cough

hotell hotel

hule n cave

hullsleiv spatula

hund dog

hurtig fast

hus house

husholdningspapir paper towel

hva what

hvem who

hver for oss separately

hvilken which

hvit white

hvitt gull white gold

hvor where

hvor langt how far

hvor lenge how long

hvor mange how many

hvor mye how much

hvor sent how late

hvordan how

hæl heel

hørselshemmet hearing impaired

høy high (tall); loud (voice)

høyde hill

høyre right (direction)

håndbagasje carry-on (luggage)

håndkle towel

håndveske handbag

hår hair

hårbalsam conditioner (hair)

hårbørste hairbrush

hårlakk hair spray

I

i in

i dag today

i går yesterday

i kveld tonight

i morgen tomorrow

i nærheten nearby

i veien wrong

ibuprofen ibuprofen (pharmaceutical)

idrett sports

idrettsmassasje sports massage

igjen left (remaining)

ikke not

ikke noe no (not anything)

ild fire (open)

imponerende impressive

informasjon information

informasjonsskranke information desk

ingen no one

ingenting nothing

inkludere v include

inkludert included

inneholde v contain

innendørs svømmebas-seng indoor pool

innenlands domestic

inngangsbillett admis-sion (price)

inngangspenger cover charge

inni inside
innkvartering accommodations (accomodation BE)
innsjekkingsskranke check-in
innsjø lake
insekt insect, bug
insektmiddel insect repellent
insektstikk insect bite
interessant interesting
interessert interested
internasjonal international
internett internet
internettkafé internet cafe

J
ja yes
jakke jacket
jazz jazz
jeg I
jente girl
jernbanestasjon train (railway BE) station
jorde field

K
kafé cafe
kald cold
kaldt icy
kam comb
kamera camera
kamp game; match (sport)
karaffel carafe
kart map
kartong carton
kasse cash desk
kaste opp v vomit
kelner waiter
kilo kilo
kilometer kilometer (kilometre BE)
kino movie theater

[cinema BE]
kirke church
kjedelig boring
kjemisk toalett chemical toilet
kjenne v know (somebody)
kjole dress
kjæreste boyfriend; girlfriend
kjøleskap refrigerator
kjøpe buy
kjøpesenter mall
kjøre v drive
kjørelengde mileage
klar ready
klassisk musikk classical music
klesbutikk clothing store
kleskode dress code
klimaanlegg air conditioning
klipp haircut
klippe n cliff; v cut (with scissors)
klokke watch
klosettpumpe plunger
knipling lace
kniv knife
kobber copper
koffert suitcase
kokemuligheter cooking facilities
kollega colleague
komfyr stove
komme v come
komme frem v arrive
komme til v get to
komme tilbake v return (come back)
konditori pastry shop
kondom condom
kone wife
konferanse conference
konferansesenter convention hall
konsert concert

kontaktlinse contact lens
kontaktlinsevæske contact lens solution
kontanter cash
konto account
kontor office
kontortid office hours
kontroll control
kopi print (photo)
kopp cup
korketrekker corkscrew
kort n card; adj short
koscher kosher
koste v cost
kredittkort credit card
krone krone (Norwegian currency)
krystall crystal
kullsyrefri non-carbonated (still BE) (drink)
kunne can; may
kurs rate (of exchange)
kveld evening
kvinne woman
kvittering receipt
kysse v kiss
kåpe coat (woman's)

L
la oss let's
la være i fred v leave alone
lag team
lage v make
lagre v save (computer)
laken sheet
laktoseintolerant lactose intolerant
land country; countryside
landekode country code
lang long
langbukser pants (trousers BE)
langsom slow
langsomt slowly
langt far
lappe v mend

lav low
lavhælt flat (shoe)
leddgikt arthritis
lege doctor
legemiddel medication
legge igjen v leave (deposit)
legitimasjon identification
leie v hire; rent
leiebil rental car
leilighet apartment
lekegrind playpen
lekeplass playground
leketøy toy
leketøybutikk toy store
lett easy; light (weight)
leve v live
levende musikk live music
levere tilbake v return (give back)
lighter lighter
like v like
lin linen (cloth)
linje line (transport); extension (phone)
liten small
liter liter
litt little; some (with singular nouns)
livbåt life boat
logge seg av log off
logge seg inn log in
logge seg på log on
lokal local
lomme pocket
lommebok wallet
lunsj lunch
lusekofte cardigan (Norwegian)
lynmelder instant messenger
lys n light; adj light (color)
lysestake candlestick
lyspære light bulb
lær leather

løse inn v cash
løype trail [piste BE]
løypekart trail map [piste map BE]
lås lock
låse seg ute v lock oneself out

M

mage stomach
magesmerte stomachache
mange many
mangle v miss
manikyr manicure
mann man
marked market
maskin machine
maskinvaskbar machine washable
massasje massage
mat food
mate v feed
med with
meget very
melkeprodukter dairy
mellomstor medium
men but
menstruasjon period (monthly)
menstruasjonssmerter menstrual cramps
meny menu
mer more
messe mass (church)
meter meter
middag dinner (meal); noon [midday BE]
midnatt midnight
midt imot opposite
midtgang aisle
mikrobølgeovn microwave
mindre less
minibank ATM
minnebrikke memory card

minutt minute
miste v lose
mobil cell [mobile BE] phone
mokkasiner loafers
moms sales tax [VAT BE]
monter display case
moped moped
mopp mop
morgen morning
morsmelkerstatning formula
moské mosque
motorbåt motorboat
motorsykkel motorcycle
motorvei highway [motorway BE]
motta v receive
mulig possible
munn mouth
museum museum
musikk music
mye much
mynt coin
mørk dark
møte meeting
møterom meeting room
møtes v meet
målebeger measuring cup
måleskje measuring spoon
måltid meal
måned month
måtte v must (have to)

N

narresmokk pacifier [dummy BE] (baby's)
nasjonalpark nature preserve
natt night
natten over overnight
nattklubb nightclub
navn name
ned down
negl nail (human)

neglefil nail file
neglesalong nail salon
nei no
neste next
noe any; anything; something
noen anyone; some (with plural nouns); someone
nord north
Norge Norway
normalbensin regular (fuel)
norsk Norwegian
nummer number (counting); size (shoes)
ny new
nybegynner novice
nyte v enjoy
nær near
nærmeste nearest
nødutgang emergency exit
nøkkel key
nøkkelkort key card
nå adv now; v reach
når when

O

olabukser jeans
om ettermiddagen p.m. (afternoon)
om kvelden p.m. (evening)
om morgenen a.m.
ombordstigning boarding
ombordstigningskort boarding pass
område area; region
opera opera
oppbevaringsboks luggage locker
opptatt busy
oppvaskmaskin dishwasher
oppvaskmiddel dish detergent [washing-up liquid BE]
optiker optician

ordbok dictionary
ostehøvel cheese slicer
overfall attack; mugging
overfalle v mug
oversette v translate
overvektig bagasje excess luggage
overveldende stunning

P

p-pille pill (contraceptive)
pakke package [parcel BE]; v pack
pakke inn v wrap up
palass palace
papir paper
papirkluter baby wipes
papirkopi av et digitalt bilde digital print
papirlommetørkle tissue
paracetamol acetaminophen [paracetamol BE]
paraply umbrella
parfyme perfume
parfymeri perfumery
park n park
parkere v park
parkeringsplass parking lot [car park BE]
pass passport
passe v fit
passende suitable
passkontroll passport control
passord password
peke v point
penger money
penicillin penicillin
penn pen
pensjonat guesthouse
pensjonert retired (from work)
pensjonist senior citizen
per dag per day

per kilometer per kilometer [kilometre BE]
per natt per night
per time per hour
per uke per week
perle pearl
perrong platform [BE] (station)
picnic picnic
pille pill
plage v bother
plaskebasseng kiddie [paddling BE] pool
plass place (hostel); seat; square
plaster bandage [plaster BE]
plastfolie plastic wrap [cling film BE]
plombe filling (tooth)
politi police
politirapport police report
politistasjon police station
popmusikk pop music
porsjon portion
post mail [post BE]
postkasse mailbox [postbox BE]
postkontor post office
postkort postcard
praktfull amazing
presentere v introduce (person)
presse v press (iron)
pris price
problem problem
protestantisk Protestant
prøve v try on
prøverom fitting room
pund pound (money)
puste v breathe
pute pillow
pyjamas pajamas
på on (place); to (time)

R
rabatt discount
racket racket (sport)
rane rob
rap rap (music)
rapport report
rask quick
regn n rain
regne v rain
regnfrakk raincoat
regnfull rainy
regning n check [bill BE] (restaurant)
reinsdyrskinn reindeer skin
reise v travel
reisebyrå travel agency
reisehåndbok travel guide
reisesjekk traveler's check [cheque BE]
reisesyke motion sickness
ren clean
rengjøringsmidler cleaning supplies
renseri dry cleaner
reparere v fix; repair
resept prescription
restaurant restaurant
retning direction
retningsnummer area code
rett dish (food); right (correct)
rett frem straight ahead
rimelig inexpensive
ring n ring (jewelry)
ringe v call (phone)
ringetid prepaid calling time
robåt rowboat
rolig quiet
rom room
romantisk romantic
romservice room service

rosa pink
ruin n ruin
rullestol wheelchair
rullestolsrampe wheelchair ramp
rulletrapp escalator
runde round (golf)
rundt around (nearby)
rute route
rutetabell schedule [timetable BE] (transportation)
rygg back (body part)
ryggsekk backpack
rød red
røyke v smoke
røykfri non-smoking (area)

S
safe n safe; adj trygg
saks scissors
salve cream (pharmaceutical)
samtale call (phone)
sandaler sandals
sanitetsbind sanitary napkin [towel BE]
savnet missing
se v look; see
seilbrett windsurfer
selge v sell
selvbetjeningsvaskeri laundromat [launderette BE]
seminar seminar
sen late
sende v send; ship
sende e-post v e-mail
senere later
seng bed
sentrum downtown area
separert separated
servere v serve
service service
serviett napkin
servitør waiter, waitress

sete ved midtgangen aisle seat
setning sentence
sette v put
sette inn v insert
sette over v put through
severdighet point of interest
shorts shorts
si v tell
side side
sigar cigar
sigarett cigarette
sightseeing sightseeing
sightseeingtur sightseeing tour
silke silk
sist last
sjampo shampoo
sjekk n check [cheque BE]
sjekke e-post v check e-mail
sjekke inn check in (airport)
sjekke ut check out
sjø sea
skade v damage
skatt tax
ski skis
skiheis ski lift
skilt divorced
skip ship
skitrekk drag lift
skitten dirty
skive slice
skje spoon
skjema form (document)
skjerf scarf
skjorte shirt
skjørt skirt
sko shoes
skobutikk shoe store
skog forest
skrive v write; type (computer)
skrive ut v print

skru av *v* turn off (device)

skru på *v* turn on (device)

skyve *v* push (open)

skål saucer; cheers (a toast)

slagsted battleground

sleiv spatula

slett *v* clear (ATM)

slette *v* delete (computer)

slott castle

slutt *n* end

slutte *v* end

smake *v* taste

smakløs bland

smerte pain

smykker jewelry

snakke *v* speak

snart soon

snorkleutstyr snorkeling equipment

snø *n/v* snow

snøbrett snowboard

sokk sock

sol sun

solbriller sunglasses

solforbrenning sunburn

solkrem sunscreen

solstikk sunstroke

sommer summer

spa spa

spasere *v* walk (stroll)

spesialitet speciality

spille *v* play

spille på hester *v* place a bet

spillehall arcade

spillkort playing card

spise *v* eat

spisekart menu (printed)

spor track (railway)

springvann tap water

sprinkelseng crib [child's cot BE]

språk language

spørre *v* ask

spørsmål question

stadion stadium

starte *v* start

stasjon station

staver poles (ski)

sted place

stekepanne frying pan

stemple stamp

stenge *v* close

stengt closed

sterlingsølv sterling silver

sti path

stikkontakt outlet (electric) [socket BE]

stjele *v* steal

stjålet stolen

stol chair

stolheis chair lift

stoppe *v* stop

stor big; large

stormagasin department store

storslagen magnificent

strand beach

strykejern iron (clothing)

strømpe stocking

strømpebukse panty hose [tights BE]

strømuttak electrical outlet

student student

studere *v* study

stuss trim (hair)

stygg ugly

stykke piece; play (theater)

style *v* style (hair)

større bigger

størrelse size (clothes)

støvel boot

støvsuger vacuum cleaner

sulten hungry

super premium; super (gasoline)

supermarked supermarket

surfebrett surfboard

surstoffbehandling oxygen treatment

suvenir souvenir

suvenirbutikk souvenir store

svart black

svelge *v* swallow

svensk Swedish

Sverige Sweden

svimmel dizzy

svømme *v* swim

svømmebasseng swimming pool

syk sick [ill BE]

sykebil ambulance

sykeforsikring health insurance

sykehus hospital

sykepleier nurse

sykkel bicycle

sykkelløp cycling race

sykkelsti bike route

sykling cycling

synagoge synagogue

synshemmet visually impaired

sølv silver

søppel trash [rubbish BE]

søppelsekk garbage [rubbish BE] bag

sør south

søt cute

søvnighet drowsiness

såpe soap

sår hals sore throat

T

T-bane subway [underground BE]

T-banestasjon subway [underground BE] station

T-skjorte T-shirt

ta *v* take

ta med *v* bring (something)

ta med seg *v* take away (carry)

ta selv *v* help (oneself)

ta ut *v* withdraw (from account)

tablett tablet (medical)

takke *v* thank

tall number (counting)

tallerken plate

tampong tampon

tann tooth

tannlege dentist

tannbørste toothbrush

tannpasta toothpaste

tannpine toothache

taubane cable car

tegn symbol

tekst *n* text (message)

tekste *v* text (someone)

telefon phone

telefonkort phone card

telefonnummer phone number

telefonsamtale phone call

telt tent

tempel temple (religion)

tenke på *v* think about

tennis tennis

tennisbane tennis court

tenniskamp tennis match

terminal terminal (airport)

teskje teaspoon

tid time

til to (direction)

til until (time)

tilbake back (direction)

tilbehør accessories

tillate *v* permit

tillatt allowed

tiltrekkende attractive

time hour; lesson

ting thing

tinn pewter

titt look

toalett restroom [toilet BE]

toalettpapir toilet paper

tobakk tobacco
tobakkshandel tobacconist's
tog train
togtabell train schedule [timetable BE]
tolk interpreter
toll customs; duty (tax)
tollfri duty-free
tom empty
topp peak
torg town square
tradisjonell traditional
trafikklys traffic light
trafikkskilt road sign
tralle cart (luggage)
trapp stairs
travbane racetrack [race course BE]
treffe v see (meet)
trefigur wooden figurine
trekke v pull
trenge v need
treningsdrakt sweatsuit
trikk tram BE
trimrom gym
tro v think (believe)
truger snowshoes
trygg safe (free from danger)
trykk pressure
trøye undershirt
trådløst internett wireless internet
tung heavy
tur tour; trip
tur-returbillett round-trip [return BE ticket]
turistklasse economy class
turistkontor tourist office
turnsko sneakers
turområde picnic area
tursti walking route

TV TV
typisk typically
tyv thief
tyveri theft
tøfler slippers
tøm v empty
tørr adj dry
tåteflaske baby bottle

U

ugift single (unmarried)
uke week
ukentlig adj weekly
ull wool
ullteppe blanket
ulykke accident
underbukse panties, drawers, shorts
underlig strange
underrette v notify
undersøke v see (examine)
undertegne v sign
ungdomsherberge youth hostel
unge kid
universitet university
unnskyld! sorry!
unnskylde v excuse
urolig mage upset stomach
uten without
utendørs svømmebasseng outdoor pool
utenfor outside
utflukt excursion, trip, outing
utgang exit; gate
utleie hire
utsikt overlook
utsjekking check out
utslett rash
utstyr equipment
uttale v pronounce; n pronunciation
uvel nauseous

V

vakker beautiful
valuta currency
vandrerhjem youth hostel
vann water
vannscooter jet ski
vannski water skis
vanskelig difficult
vare goods
varm hot; warm
varme n heat (heating BE); v warm
varmeovn heater
vask laundry (clothes)
vaskbar washable
vaske v clean; wash
vaskemaskin washing machine
vaskemiddel detergent
vaskemuligheter laundry facilities
ved prep at, by, on n firewood
ved siden av next to
vegetarianer vegetarian
vei road
veikart road map
veikryss intersection
vekke v wake
vekking wake-up call
veksle v change (money); exchange
vekslepenger n change (money)
vekslingskontor currency exchange office
vekslingskurs exchange rate
velkommen welcome
venn friend
venstre left
vente v wait
vente på v wait for
verdi value
vest west

vifte fan (appliance)
vikingskip viking ship
viktig important
ville want to
vindu window
vindusplass window seat
vinkart wine list
vinmonopol liquor store [off-licence BE]
vinter winter
virke v work (function)
vise v show
visittkort business card
vite v know (something)
voldtekt rape
volleyballkamp volleyball game
vondt i brystet chest pain
vær så snill please
vær weather
være v be
værutsikter weather forecast

Ø

ørering earring
øreverk earache
øst east
øye eye
øyeblikk moment
øyeblikkelig quickly
øyenbryn eyebrow
øyenskygge eye shadow
øyensverte mascara
øyenvitne eye witness

Å

åpen adj open
åpne v open
åpningstid v business hours
år year
årstid season
åtti eighty

INDEX

Berlitz pocket guide

NORWAY

Third Edition 2018

Editor: Ros Walford
Author: Anna Espsäter
Head of Production: Rebeka Davies
Picture Editor: Tom Smyth
Cartography Update: Carte
Update Production: Apa Digital
Photography Credits: Alamy 1, 53, 70; Andreas Gruhle/visitnorway.com 41; Bård Løken/Visitnorway.com 12; Erik Christensen 17; Getty Images 24, 97; Glyn Genin/Apa Publications 14, 21, 29, 32, 37, 38, 57, 58, 61, 71, 75, 76, 83, 89, 90, 91; Hurtigruten 4TC, 7, 7R; Ian Brodie/visitrjukan.com 34; Innovation Norge 48, 50, 54, 64, 74, 80, 84, 85, 86, 93, 98, 101; iStock 4MC, 4ML, 5T, 5M, 5M, 11, 26, 42, 45, 46, 73, 79; Public domain 18; Shutterstock 4TL, 5TC, 63, 66, 69; Staib Heiner/Hurtigruten 6R; Tina Stafrèn/Visitnorway.com 102, 104; Trym Ivar Bergsmo/Hurtigruten 6L; VISITOSLO/Munchmuseet 5MC; VISITOSLO/Tord Baklund 30; Øyvind Blomstereng/My Magical Moments/Visitnorway.com 5MC
Cover Picture: Shutterstock

Distribution
UK, Ireland and Europe: Apa Publications (UK) Ltd; sales@insightguides.com
United States and Canada: Ingram Publisher Services; ips@ingramcontent.com
Australia and New Zealand: Woodslane; info@woodslane.com.au
Southeast Asia: Apa Publications (SN) Pte; singaporeoffice@insightguides.com
Worldwide: Apa Publications (UK) Ltd; sales@insightguides.com

Special Sales, Content Licensing and CoPublishing
Insight Guides can be purchased in bulk quantities at discounted prices. We can create special editions, personalised jackets and corporate imprints tailored to your needs. sales@insightguides.com; www.insightguides.biz

Contact us
Every effort has been made to provide accurate information in this publication, but changes are inevitable. The publisher cannot be responsible for any resulting loss, inconvenience or injury. We would appreciate it if readers would call our attention to any errors or outdated information. We also welcome your suggestions; please contact us at: berlitz@apaguide.co.uk
www.insightguides.com/berlitz

Berlitz®

speaking your language

phrase book & dictionary
phrase book & CD

Available in: Arabic, Brazilian Portuguese*, Burmese*, Cantonese Chinese, Croatian, Czech*, Danish*, Dutch, English, Filipino, Finnish*, French, German, Greek, Hebrew*, Hindi*, Hungarian*, Indonesian, Italian, Japanese, Korean, Latin American Spanish, Malay, Mandarin Chinese, Mexican Spanish, Norwegian, Polish, Portuguese, Romanian*, Russian, Spanish, Swedish, Thai, Turkish, Vietnamese
*Book only